God that's not Fair

"Since this book was first published, there has been increasing debate amongst Christians about the nature of hell. This is an important issue and the debate must continue. But there is a great danger. Will the subject just be an issue for debate? Dick Dowsett insists that the eternal judgement of the non-Christian is a tragedy that must be faced and is a reality which must dramatically affect the life of every Christian."

Peter Maiden, Associate International Director of Operation Mobilisation

God that's not Fair

Understanding Eternal Punishment
and the Christian's Urgent Mission

Dick Dowsett

OM
publishing

Copyright © 1982 Overseas Missionary Fellowship,
OMF Books, Belmont, The Vine, Sevenoaks TN13 3TZ, U.K.

Reprinted in association with OMF Books in the UK 1993 by OM Publishing.
This edition 1998.

04 03 02 01 00 99 98   7 6 5 4 3 2 1

OM Publishing is an imprint of Paternoster Publishing,
P.O. Box 300, Carlisle, Cumbria, CA3 0QS, U.K.
http://www.paternoster-publishing.com

British Library Cataloguing in Publication Data
A catalogue record for this book is available from the British Library.

ISBN 0 85078 284 9

All biblical quotations are taken from the Revised Standard Version unless otherwise stated.

Cover design by Mainstream, Lancaster
Printed in Great Britain by Mackays of Chatham PLC, Kent

CONTENTS

FOREWORD

Much thought has gone into the question of what motivates people to a vision for world mission. Gratitude for the love of Christ, desire for the welfare of men, a sense of duty both to God and neighbour — these and many other stimuli have sent men out into the world for Jesus Christ. But we today have often neglected three areas of motivation which were of particular significance in the past.

When Christians see the overall pattern of God's activity for the nations of the world throughout history, they begin to see the plan of God for their own lives within that greater divine purpose. In the Old Testament God called Israel so to demonstrate God's glory in her communal national life that the other nations would be attracted to Jehovah. In the New Testament the church is called not only to show forth God's greatness by her life, but also to move out to all nations in verbal proclamation. We are part of God's plan in history.

Secondly, the Puritans and many others were moved to world mission by their sure hope that the world is heading for a great climax when the fullness of the Gentiles will be gathered in and also all Israel will be saved (Romans 11.25-26).

They looked forward with eager anticipation to the day when the earth will be filled with the knowledge of the glory of the Lord, as the waters cover the sea (Hab. 2.14). The Lord will 'ransom men for God from every tribe and tongue and people and nation' (Rev. 5.9) and we as Christians are called to work towards this exciting future. I look forward to someone writing a new book to open up this eschatological hope, which has played such a key role in sending men and women to all parts of the world for Jesus Christ.

It is the third area of motivation which Dick Dowsett has tackled in this book with his inimitable enthusiasm and flair for easy communication. Through a series of letters from a young Christian, and Dick's answers, we are led into the whole subject of eternal judgment and Hell. Many of the great missionary pioneers went to the far corners of the world because they had caught the vision of people heading for eternity without Christ and in total separation from God. Many today find this hard to accept and react, 'God, that's not fair!' Dick shows not only that it's fair, but that if we really believe it then in love we must warn those in danger of the fearful judgment ahead; to leave them in ignorance would indeed be a kind of murder.

This book is not intended to be a heavy theological work and it is possible that it will not totally satisfy those who are looking for weighty discussion of current theological questions such as the possibility of revelation and salvation outside the Christian faith. This is meant to be a popular book for thinking Christians — and it succeeds!

I rejoice in the courage of OMF in commissioning a book on the very controversial and highly important issue of eternal judgment. It is good that this topic was placed in the capable hands of a man like Dick Dowsett who has considerable experience overseas as a missionary, who knows well the thinking of students and young Christians in Britain, who communicates with such winsome and loving sincerity and who is clearly rooted in Scripture with an obvious love for Jesus Christ.

It is my real pleasure and privilege to commend this book most warmly. I trust it will be widely read and will help many to face up to its subject matter in the clear light of Scripture. I am confident that it will play a definite part in reemphasising this fundamental motivation for mission. May the Spirit of Jesus therefore send forth a growing stream of men and women into Christian mission in every continent and country.

Martin Goldsmith,
All Nations Christian College

PREFACE

This has been a difficult book to write. Some of my friends seem wonderfully able to dash off manuscripts during a few days break from normal work. Another produces great stuff in the wee small hours and speaks seriously of the blessings of insomnia. But writing does not come easily to me. I'm a preacher and perhaps a counsellor, but not an author. So the insistent request to write this book did not and still does not meet with an enthusiastic response from me.

But the problem was multiplied when the subject was given. Whoever wants to write a book on Hell? There is no more unpalatable subject in Christian theology!

There has been a widespread running away from the fact of Hell and what it means, even in evangelical circles, recently. People long for the assurance of Heaven, but they do not want to face up to the horrors of the alternative destination. But the two stand or fall together. As John Wesley wrote to William Law in 1756, 'If there be no unquenchable fire, no everlasting burnings, there is no dependence on those writings wherein they are so expressly asserted, nor of the eternity of Heaven any more than of Hell. So that if we give up the one, we must give up the other. No Hell, no Heaven, no revelation!'

The fate of the lost is not the only motive for world mission. It is, however, a factor that has always given urgency to the missionary task. But today more and more Christians are oblivious of the danger that rests over the heads of the un-evangelized. They live under the sick illusion that there is a back door into Heaven, or some other way that they can be saved. The Great Commission is reduced to, 'Go into all the world and make disciples of all nations, and if you don't manage it, I died for them anyway, so it will be all right somehow.'

So then, it's not surprising that with Hell forgotten, the social, economic, and political needs of the nations are given more immediate importance than their need to hear the Gospel and be converted. The result is that even in a mission like OMF, the bulk of the enquiries which we receive for service are not for our primary goal of evangelizing Asians. And the big shortage of workers is for church planters and evangelists.

I believe that there is a need for this doctrine to be tackled more fully for the sort of people who like to toss ideas backwards and forwards in theological colleges and seminaries. I have not written this book for that market, largely because I believe that theology divorced from life and pastoral practice (as it often is in theological colleges) is not, and cannot be, true biblical theology. Biblical truth has been given to change lives, not simply to stimulate discussion.

Because I wanted to write a book for ordinary people interacting with the questions, problems and doubts that ordinary people express, I've written in the form of a correspondence with a young Christian friend called Paul. The correspondence is imaginary in that Paul, with his friends and family, exists only in my mind. His questions and problems typify many that have been brought to me over the years in which I have sought to share a burden for world mission. The details from our own family life are real enough! And there is nothing imaginary about the biblical problems we grapple with.

It is my prayer that this book will not be used as fuel for argument. I long rather that it might have a small contribution in the raising up of men and women who will be prepared to risk their lives to share the Gospel — the only antidote to Hell — with the incredible numbers who have still not heard.

Dick Dowsett
Glasgow, June 1982.

1

APPROACHING THE PROBLEM

Dear Paul,

I was delighted to receive your explosive letter this morning. There are few more disheartening experiences than standing at a church door receiving warm handshakes and empty comments about the 'nice sermon'. But you were angry with my message on Sunday night. At last something is getting through!

And I can hardly blame you for getting mad about it, because I don't like what I had to say either. But for all your protests, I have to say it again: *Every person who is not a real Christian is in great danger, lost and Hell-bound*. And that is not emphasized for fun. I don't like it any more than you do. But it is urgent if it is true — and I believe it is.

In fact that is the real question. Is it true? Too often the questions we ask are 'Do I like it?', 'Does it make me feel good?'

Imagine someone has just been told he has cancer of the stomach. He will be a strange character if he bubbles with delight at the news. Most probably he will feel pretty depressed about the diagnosis. I suppose he could opt to live in a pretend world where cancer does not exist. He might *feel* better by denying the truth of his condition, but he

would not *be* better. His hope really lies in
accepting the diagnosis and undergoing
appropriate treatment.

According to the Bible, the majority of
people are 'on the road to destruction' —
terminally ill with the most desperate disease.
As I put it in my sermon, 98% of the people
in Asia are a write-off. And they make up
half the world's population. If that is true,
then desperate treatment is urgently needed at
once. And nobody is really helped by denying
it (even if you may sleep better as a result).

The fact is that more and more Christians
in Britain do not believe it. Many argue that
the 'good Muslim' and his like is acceptable to
God. Many are persuaded that there is a
second chance for those who have never
heard the Gospel. Many simply do not believe
in Hell. And others who keep it in their creed
deny it in their practice, reducing mission to
social work with a Christian smile. We do not
fulfil the Great Commission to take the
Gospel to every creature if we only dig wells,
train in self-help projects, and feed the
hungry.

In my work of encouraging and processing
missionary candidates for East Asia, I am glad
about every one who offers for medical work,
every university lecturer prepared to face the
rigours of the tropics, every teacher who is
willing to train our missionaries' children. The
heartache is that there is not nearly a
comparable number who want to go to Asia

with the primary aim of sharing the Gospel with Asians.

The conclusion is inescapable. Most Christians today — even the evangelicals — do not believe that non-Christians are lost and need to be saved.

Now, Paul, are they right — or wrong? What is the truth about people? Do you find it by seeing what most people believe? The majority used to think that the world was flat. But it wasn't! There is no real reason to believe that today's majority opinions are any more reliable.

Of course the problem for the people in the Middle Ages was that they just could not get to look at the earth from the right perspective. They did not have the equipment to learn the right answers. And their presuppositions were against them getting there anyway.

That is the problem today with this question of how God regards the unbeliever. The best of us only have a worm's-eye-view of God. And most people have presuppositions that rule certain options out of court. How often have you heard people say: 'My God would never send anyone to Hell' or 'I cannot conceive of a God of love acting in that way'?

When people in Old Testament times said they could not conceive of a God who would do this or that, the prophetic reply was: 'My thoughts are not your thoughts, neither are your ways my ways, says the LORD. For as the

heavens are higher than the earth, so are my
ways higher than your ways and my thoughts
than your thoughts' (Isaiah 55.8f). In other
words, human hunches do not give us right
answers about God. Neither can we learn how
God would behave by looking at the way that
nice people do things.

If we want to know what God thinks of the
unbeliever, and what He will do, then God
has got to tell us.

When you trusted Jesus as your Saviour and
Lord and God and became a Christian, you
were not merely affirming that Jesus was a
pretty good guy. He is God, and therefore
supremely knows what He is talking about.
You believed He had the right answers.

Do you remember the struggle you had
trying to fit your avant-garde ideas with the
Jesus sex-ethic? What an upheaval it was for
you to agree with Jesus about that! Do you
remember how we talked long into the night
over the problems that would come if you
agreed with Jesus? Your whole life-style
revolved around values and relationships
which you could not keep if you were going to
follow Jesus. It cost you a lot to get that right.
Wasn't it worth it?

Now, you have got to face what Jesus says
about God and the unbeliever. He doesn't
have our worm's-eye-view of things (John
3.11-13, 31). He knows what He is talking
about. And there is more about Hell in the
gospels than anywhere else in the Bible. But I

think you need to look right through your
Bible. For Jesus not only taught what is true.
He also made it clear that He regards all that
the Old Testament says as God's own words
— stamped with His reliability.[1]

Why not try starting with Genesis, and
work through God's thoughts on just how lost
people are? I reckon you will be in for just as
much trauma as you had over the sex issue,
because from what you have written I know
that many of your values and relationships
will be radically changed by this study. Unless
of course you want to argue with the Word of
God as well as with me . . .

Do write and argue it out with me as much
as you like. But if you see it in black and
white in the Scripture, then you disagree at
your own risk.

Cancers need to be treated — not to be
argued against!

I look forward to hearing from you soon.
Rosemary and the kids are all keeping pretty
well. The boys are missing Uncle Hon
Leong's judo lessons but seem to be picking
up other self-defence techniques native to
Glasgow! We appreciate your prayers for their
sanctification — and ours!

Every blessing,
DICK.

---

[1] A helpful study book on the reliability of the Old
Testament is *Christ and the Bible*, by J W Wenham
(IVP).

2

THE START OF IT ALL

Dear Dick,

Thank you for your letter and for your insistence that I should give myself to wholehearted Bible study on this vexed subject. I agree that I've got to learn to think the way that God thinks. And I'm prepared to concede that perhaps some of my gut reactions are less truly Christian than I would like to believe. I still do not like what you have said and find it terribly hard to believe that the God who has loved me and brought such joy to my life could be so terrible in judgment on the unevangelized.

For all that, I have started the Bible study that you suggest and begun at the beginning with the first parts of Genesis.

Honestly, I can't see that the Garden of Eden is relevant to the discussion. I wouldn't have thought that any educated person these days accepted this story as being really true. I got certain helpful thoughts for myself out of it when I first read it in my quiet time. But I can't see that it has anything to say about world evangelization, still less about the fate of those who have never heard the Gospel. I can acknowledge that these chapters have devotional value for us Western Christians. But I doubt if they make any real contribution to the discussion that we're involved in.

Forgive a short note. The firm have asked me to take a few courses. Some of them are in the evening and they are giving me time out for the others. But it is making life a bit hectic at the moment. Looking forward to hearing from you soon.

PAUL.

Dear Paul,

I'm sorry that you do not think the Garden of Eden is relevant to the discussion. Jesus certainly did not regard it as an old wives' tale! Instead He argued that what you learn from that story about the way men and women are made is still relevant today (see Matthew 19. 4-6).

Jesus, and the New Testament writers as a whole, taught that Adam was not simply a pattern of the average Western Christian. He was 'the first man' and he 'fell' as the father of the human race. Check up, by reading Romans 5.12ff, 1 Cor. 15.45,49. When Adam disobeyed God he mucked things up for everybody who was to follow.

My daughter Rachel has got my flirtatious blue eyes, my wife's stubbornness, and my temper! We do not have to understand all the mysteries of what we get from our parents'

genes or what we get from the environment in
which we live, to appreciate that nobody born
since Adam has come unprogrammed into the
world. We all start bent, with plenty to urge
and encourage us in a sinful direction. The
problem is our descent from Adam. So we
have to say that every person here in our
country is descended from Adam and is
gripped by the results of the Fall; but that is
also true of everyone elsewhere too.

So you're right in thinking that there's a
sense in which Adam is just like you. But that
is only true if you don't leave it there. He is
just like you because he's just like everyone
else in his fallen state.

When you see that, you should be able to
appreciate the importance of these first three
chapters of the Bible. They give us the
blueprint of what people are meant to be like.
They also show us what's wrong with people
at rock-bottom.

Now perhaps we can look at these chapters
from the standpoint of our problem — the
fate of the heathen.

God made people to be specially valuable
— 'in the image of God'. All over the world
people have lost that sense of value.

When I first went to the Philippines in 1968
there were more guns than people. Every day
the tabloid newspapers had a mangled corpse
on the front page. My wife's uncle, the
captain of an oil tanker, said Manila was the
only port in the Free World where it was too

dangerous to allow his seamen ashore! People had become a disposable commodity. During the same period we revelled in the exploits of James Bond, who shot people and used women as though they were of no more value than a Kleenex tissue.

Chinese estimates are that thirty million people had to die in order that China could become a Communist State. Most Western estimates are higher than that. Mao Tse Tung had taught that the death of an opponent of the revolution was 'lighter than a feather'. People always lose their significance in revolutionary bloodshed.

In a recent railway accident in India, thousands plunged to their death. Newspapers reported that there had been a cow on the track. The Hindu driver apparently set higher value on the life of one cow than on the survival of a train load of people. But it is people, not cows, who are made in the image of God.

An English couple I heard of recently, spoiled their old mother's home of everything of value. Then they shoved her into an old people's home and told her they hoped she would not live long. They needed her money!

What a lost place this world is. Where is the special value of each individual? God made each one to be precious, but all over the world this sense of value has been lost.

Perhaps the thing above everything else that shows the real value of people is the realization that we are made for a personal relationship with God. Here in Scotland our Shorter Catechism defines the chief end of man as 'To glorify God and to enjoy him forever'. Adam was created to go for walks with his God, to have fellowship with Him, to work with Him, to control the environment with Him, to have relationships with other people with Him. The plan was that man should enjoy life to the full with God.

Since people are designed to share with God Himself, it is hardly surprising that all over the world we find people, sometimes wistfully and usually misguidedly, seeking after a relationship with God. It is not that they hanker after this because they are inadequate, as some Freudians might suggest. The fact is that people *are* inadequate if they do not have a relationship with God. A car with an empty tank may be an interesting museum piece, but it will not fulfil the purpose for which it was made. People often lead interesting lives without God. Some of them find a place in our history books. But no one can fulfil the real purpose for his life, if he is not filled with the Spirit of God.

It is clear from Genesis that all the other purposes God has for people are meant to grow out of this fundamental relationship with Himself. And if most people in the world are at odds with God, they are bound to go wrong on all the other purposes, one way and another.

For example, God made people for satisfying and meaningful work with Him.

The God of the Bible is no passive layabout. He is a God who works! So it is that people with nothing to do and no purpose in their lives lose something of their special humanness. That is a particularly moving thing to write to you at a time when China is reporting fifty million unemployed, twenty five per cent of the Filipino work force has nothing to do, and British unemployment figures have passed the three million mark.

Some people talk as though work were a curse to be avoided at all costs. One night at a cocktail party my wife was chatting with a diplomat's wife. There in Asia she was spending her day reading paperbacks and attending parties, protected from housework by a bevy of maids. She sadly commented 'I always longed for a life of leisure. Now I've got it and it's Hell!'

We are made for the dignity of work. The boys who scavenge among the rubbish dumps of Manila have a dignity (as well as an important ecological contribution) which is often tragically eroded in our passive dole queues. They have got meaningful work — even if it is full of germs and involves long hours for small returns.

But with this almost universal problem of unemployment, more and more people are wondering what on earth they are living for. There seems to be little point to life and

nothing of great value to do. And this sense
of the pointlessness of life is not simply to be
found among the unemployed. People with
work, but with no living relationship with
God, often have that same sense of
aimlessness.

It is always a delight for me to have
fellowship with Professor Wong Hee Aik, of
the Department of Biochemistry at Singapore
University. A brilliant scientist, she has
sometimes found that other scientists of
international standing fail to take her seriously
on seeing her deceptively young looks (and
the fact that she's a woman!). They usually
change their minds when they see her results!
Her secret, she gladly shares, is that she
works together with God. She testifies to the
promptings and insights received in her
research in answer to prayer.

Whatever our work, it makes a huge
difference when we are sure we are in the job
for which we are designed, doing it with the
God who made us.

Can't you remember how excited you were
when you first discovered Ephesians 2.10?
God has work for you to do — definite plans
for your life. He made you a Christian so that
you would not miss His plan, His best work
for you.

When the time came for you to leave
school, didn't we pray? What was God's job
for you? Once you told me you would never
have stuck at it if you had not been sure that

it was God's appointment, for which you were designed. When you moved up north, you found that church where the opening came for you to lead the young people's Bible study, and as that group blossomed you saw God's purpose in that seemingly unwelcome move. It makes such a difference living with the Lord, and working for Him.

But most of the people you see each day and look at on television do not live with the Lord, do not work with Him, and haven't the faintest idea what they are here for. That is part of being lost.

Think of all those wasted lives. Does it then surprise you that one New Testament picture of Hell is of a blazing rubbish dump?

I must stop now. A Bible College student considering a call to Japan has just dropped in. How super to find someone burdened to evangelize that land. The Japanese seem to know plenty about work (and conquering our markets). But so few know anything of the living God, and 65% of their towns have no Christians at all. Believing as I do, I must spend more time with this fellow now. I'm sure you'll understand. We'll carry on with Genesis some other time.

I'm so glad your firm is giving you time out for study. I hope you will still have time to write to us with all the extra work you'll have to do.

God bless you and guide you,
DICK.

3

ISN'T SINCERITY ENOUGH?

Dear Dick,
*I was discussing some of your views about Hell
with a friend of mine who is very interested in
comparative religion. He very vigorously
disagreed with what you have said. He
reckoned that if there is a Hell, and he is
prepared to admit that there may well be, then
it would only be occupied by a very few
people. He was particularly put out by what
you think about other religions. And he
certainly seems to know what he is talking
about on that score.*

*Firstly, he argued that it is wrong to criticize
those whose religion is primitive and simple.
After all, we all started as animists. It is just
that some societies have evolved to a more
mature belief in one God. You can no more
blame people for having a primitive religion
than you can blame them for living in mud
huts or for wearing G strings.*

*Then he lectured me at great length about
the high and beautiful ideals of the major
religions of the world. And he was indeed able
to show me many beautiful things that I had
not known about. For example, the Buddhist*

ethic as practised in Thailand and many other countries is simply,

> *Do not take life.*
> *Do not take what has not been given.*
> *Do not do what is sexually immoral.*
> *Do not lie.*
> *Do not get drunk.*

There is not really a great deal of difference between that and the ten commandments, is there?

Because of these very good points in other religions, my friend argues that we are basically heading in the same direction. Therefore it is both futile and indeed downright bad manners to seek to persuade people to change their religion. If we are really going to show proper respect then our missionary work will help the good Muslim to be a better Muslim and the good Hindu to become a better Hindu.

In some ways this seems to me to be eminently reasonable. After all, the real problem of Christianity here in Britain is that so many who call themselves Christians neither understand the real thing nor practise it. If those who called themselves Christians really followed the teaching of Jesus, it would make an enormous difference. Cannot the same be said about nominal Buddhism and Islam too? The real thing is so much better than the half-hearted versions most people practise.

I hope you don't think I am wasting your time raising questions like this. I know in

*advance that you are going to disapprove of
these arguments. In a way, I disapprove of
them too. The trouble is that when they were
all thrown at me the other day I just did not
know how to answer them. And I think that I
really do need to be able to answer such
important objections if I am going to continue
thinking in the way you have so far outlined.
So I would appreciate your thoughts on this
when you get a moment.*

*I'd better stop. I'm leading the Bible Study
tonight, so I must start cramming at once. I
think that is more urgent than writing more
news. And after the way you bashed me with
2 Timothy 2.15 when I once suggested
preparation was not all that important, I know
you'll approve if I sign off now!*

*Looking forward to hearing from you soon.
PAUL.*

Dear Paul,

Thank you for your letter. I am really glad
you are taking me up on the offer to write
about the objections you have come across on
this whole subject of the fate of those who are
not real Christians. Many people just try and
sweep their doubts and questions under the
carpet. But they need to be faced and dealt
with, not left to breed and multiply in the

dark. And since God's Word does have a lot
to say about other religions and those who
sincerely practise them, it is especially
important that we should be provoked to
search this out.

However, I was a little concerned at your
tendency to play off what you call 'my
opinion' against 'his opinion'. The important
thing is to be clear as to what is *God's*
'opinion'. What *I* think about the heathen
really doesn't matter one little bit. What
matters is what the Word of God says. And if
you are to be properly Christian in your
thinking, then you will be prepared to throw
out both what I say and what he says if it
does not fit with what the Bible says.

I have certainly had to change my ideas a
lot as I have studied the Bible. But I
recognize that I still do not have all the
answers and may from time to time interpret
Scripture the wrong way. If you can show me
that, then I shall have to change my views.
But meantime let me take you through some
of the teaching of Scripture regarding the
points that you have raised.

It is tempting indeed to think that Hell
should be largely uninhabited. The problem
is, Jesus never gives that impression at all.
Rather He says,
'Enter by the narrow gate; for the gate is wide
and the way is easy, that leads to destruction,
and those who enter by it are *many*. For the
gate is narrow and the way is hard, that leads

to life, and those who find it are *few*'
(Matthew 7.13-14).

In the same sermon He said that on the day
of judgment He would declare to *'many'* 'I
never knew you; depart from me, you evil
doers' (Matthew 7.22-23). Much of the agony
of both Old and New Testaments is the
terrible lostness of so many people.

But the question that you raise in your
letter and that I want to discuss at some
length is this whole matter of other religions.

There is something very moving about
seeing films of people practising their religion.
So often there is an emotion and sincerity that
makes some of our polite, soul-less, half-
hearted Christian worship look a miserable
second best. Indeed, I feel it is a great scandal
that much that is supposed to be Christian
worship ends up as a jolly good advertisement
for other religions!

But the question is not whether a sincere
Buddhist commitment is more likely to save
than nominal Christianity. The proper
question to ask is, how can a man be made
right with God? And what is the worship that
He accepts?

Your friend's idea that primitive man is an
animist and only the more sophisticated
peoples believe that there is only one God, is
rubbish. He wants to excuse tribal and other
people for dealing with spirits on the grounds
that they are simply underdeveloped. Genesis
4 tells the story of primitive man and his worship.

'In the course of time Cain brought to the
LORD an offering of the fruit of the ground,
and Abel brought of the firstlings of his flock
and of their fat portions. And the LORD had
regard for Abel and his offering, but for Cain
and his offering he had no regard' (Genesis
4.3-5).

Primitive man dealt with the Lord —
animism came later. And there is
anthropological evidence for this too.

It is argued in the New Testament in
Romans 1 (from verse 18) that man-made
religions and the worship of created beings
(which must of course include spirits) are
culpable ungodliness. The reason is that man
has turned from the God who is obviously
there.

I must confess that I used to think the
apostle Paul was writing from an ignorant and
bigoted Jewish position and that he ought to
have had much more sympathy for other
religions. Now, however, I am persuaded to
take the apostle Paul more seriously and to
give less credit to those anthropologists who
disagree with him.

Very many animistic cultures have an
awareness of God over all. For all that, they
deal with lesser beings like spirits and
demons. So, many animists in the Philippines
do know of 'Bathala', the Supreme Being.
But by now, the concept of the Lord has
become rather distorted. Even at the human
level, if you don't bother to keep up with a

friend and lose touch for many years, then your ideas about him become very blurred and quite distorted. So it is with people who have known of God but not dealt with Him.

Friends of mine who worked with the Hmong tribe in Asia tell me that these people have a word for 'God'. But the missionaries are loath to use it in evangelism because it is full of unbiblical ideas. So it is better to use a completely different word for God rather than to use their word with all the wrong ideas bound up with it. And yet, even that problem bears out the argument of Romans 1 that people have pushed under what they did know about the true God. They knew God, they did not honour him as God, so their ideas became distorted.

You will remember that when Paul went to Athens he observed that they had an altar 'to an unknown god'. Evidently the Athenians knew that there was a God somewhere whom they did not know. But they did know that they needed to be right with Him.

The knowledge of God has been enthusiastically pushed under by sinful peoples of every race and culture. But it still lurks in the background, a confused, blurred image. And a warning witness too.

Whenever I look at religious practice around the world I am struck by the strange mixture of right and wrong that one finds all over the place. It is not that everything in all other religions is totally wrong. The Buddhist ethic you quoted in your letter is something that we would want to agree with. However, we might become rather unhappy if we were to ask how the standard is to be achieved, or what are the incentives to aim at it. Similarly, we may in some measure approve of the Muslim's concept of Hell. But we would be rather unwilling to accept his way of salvation from it.

In other words the doctrine of 'total depravity' relates to world religions as much as to anything else. The religions contain what we might call good bits mixed up with the bad. But even the good bits are spoilt by sinful thinking.

People who argue in favour of other religions are often right to show us the common ground that they have with Christianity. Sadly, they do not like it when we ask questions about the way that these lovely elements fit in with the whole scheme of the religion.

If we go back to Cain and Abel for a moment we shall see this very well illustrated. You will remember that they both brought an offering to the Lord. Neither of them reckoned to walk into the presence of God just as he was. That is good thinking. They had grasped a truth which has been very important since the days the gate to the Garden of Eden was shut. When Adam had lived there he did not bring an offering when he came to have fellowship with God. There

was no need, for there was no guilt in his
heart and no sin to arouse the wrath of God.

But once the gate into Eden was closed by
our sin, people could no longer come to God
just as they are. A sacrifice is needed. Both
Cain and Abel realized this, and so do most
religious people in the world today. Most
people do not understand the doctrine of
propitiation,[1] but they do know that they
cannot come to God just as they are. So we
find the religions of the world going to great
lengths in all sorts of sacrifices, painful
penances or expensive animal offerings.

Now it is a profound truth that the wrath of
God needs to be propitiated if people are
going to enjoy His presence. But the question
that we have to ask is 'How is the wrath of
God propitiated?' The Christian answer is
'without the shedding of blood there is no
forgiveness of sins' (Hebrews 9.22), and that
the only shed blood which really deals with
the problem is the blood of Jesus our Saviour.
The Old Testament sacrifices were a picture
of this.

When we look at the story of Cain and
Abel we find that the Lord accepted the lamb
that Abel brought, but rejected the fruit Cain
offered. I remember as a child seeing a film of
the early parts of the Bible. In the film, the
smoke from Abel's sacrifice went straight up

---

[1] 'Propitiation' means 'the removal of wrath by the
offering of a gift.' See 1 John 2.2, where NIV
translates it 'atoning sacrifice'.

to Heaven, but the smoke from Cain's sacrifice blew back in his face. That was dramatic guess-work. I do not know how God assured Abel that his sacrifice was acceptable, but He did. He also made it clear to Cain that he was not accepted. In other words, Cain knew he had to bring a sacrifice, but the sacrifice that he brought did not achieve peace with God.

The New Testament reminded early Jewish Christians of their previous religious background: 'Every priest stands daily at his service, offering repeatedly the same sacrifices, which can never take away sins' (Hebrews 10.11). The old Jewish sacrifices pointed forward to the people's need of the sacrificial death of Jesus as their representative and substitute. But only Jesus could do the job. Only He can 'by a single offering' perfect 'for all time those who are (being) sanctified' (Hebrews 10.14). What was true of Jewish sacrifices is true of the sacrifices of other religions too, though in a more blurred and confused way. They point to the need of the perfect Saviour and His sacrifice for sin. They do not, and can never, take away sin themselves.

Cain was right that he needed to come with a sacrifice, but he was wrong about the sacrifice that was needed.

You know, of course, that many of the sacrifices done in the world are not done for God. Rather they are attempts to appease

spirits which have been offended. The
Sagadas of the Northern Philippines will
sacrifice up to eighteen pigs and eleven
chickens during the terminal illness and time
following the death of an adult member of the
group. There is a special concern to satisfy the
spirits of the ancestors. A friend of mine told
me recently that it is arguable that Thailand
could be set on its feet economically if people
were not to spend so much money on spirit
offerings and merit-making sacrifices.

Any old sacrifice just will not do. It does
not save, and it often leads to economic
hardship as well.

Another thing to notice about the first
'other religion' in the Bible is that it did not
change Cain's life. Often we are told that
people worship God in the way they find most
helpful. 'If they find it helpful to pray in front
of a big image, who am I to say that it is
wrong to do so?'

But the fact is that God doesn't look at
things that way. When the people made the
golden calf in the wilderness they were
adopting something out of Baalism that
appealed to them. But they still claimed to be
worshipping Yahweh, the Lord. When the
people brought the image of the calf to Aaron
he encouraged them to use it for a 'feast to
the LORD' (Exodus 32.5). It could be argued
that they found this more tangible symbol of
God helpful to their worship. They were a
simple people who could not cope with an

invisible God. But the calf was borrowed from
Baalism, and along with it came fertility cult
forms of worship. Their feast to the Lord
'turned into an orgy of drinking and sex'
(Exodus 32.6, Good News Bible).

Moses, the friend of God, who really was in
touch with the attitude of the Lord about all
this, was furious. The question is not, 'Do the
people like it?' The question is, 'Is God
pleased?' And in this case He was not. He
said that His wrath 'burned hot' against them!
Their religion did not make them like God: it
made God mad at them.

This sort of divine intolerance tends to stick
in our throats. Why shouldn't people take the
best out of all the religions they encounter?
Why shouldn't we be free to pick and choose
things that we find most helpful?

The fact is that what really counts with us is
sincerity. With God, what matters is truth and
obedience.

Some years ago my brother felt sick and
had a backache. My mother called the doctor
and he said it was probably just some minor
sickness. He prescribed bed rest and aspirins.
I do not doubt the sincerity of his diagnosis
and prescription. But my mother was
concerned to have a second opinion. Another
doctor was called who diagnosed polio and
had my brother moved to hospital at once.
The next day he was paralysed from the waist
downwards. But he was in the right place for
good treatment and lives a normal healthy life

today. If we had followed the sincere advice
of the first doctor he would probably have
died.

Sincerity is not enough. One may be
sincerely wrong. And the results can be fatal.

I think it might be easy to look at God's
intolerance of other religions and picture Him
as a sort of vindictive old man in the sky who
says, 'You do it my way, or you're damned!' I
do in fact believe that God would be only just
and right to condemn us all eternally. But the
reason for intolerance about other religions is
not simply a cold clinical interest in truth.
God's intolerance is also rooted in His
compassion. He is fundamentally opposed to
other religions *BECAUSE THEY DO NOT
WORK*.

I always used to be rather embarrassed at
the way that Paul told the Galatians to
condemn anyone who came preaching a
different message from his own. He even said
that if he came back with a changed message
they should kick him out too! The reason was
not one of pig-headed bigotry, though. It is
simply that there is no other Good News.
There isn't any other message that brings
salvation. There isn't any other Gospel.

And this is the trouble. From Cain
onwards, wrong religion has not worked. Cain
had no answer to the jealousy and murder
that lurked in his heart. His religion did not
ease his conscience, did not encourage him in
his relationships with others, left him

wandering in the Land of Nod with no real meaning to his life, and did nothing to reconcile him to God. It may have begun as sincere religion. But because it was wrong, it didn't work.

Now this is the big thrust of the sarcastic arguments that Isaiah brings against other religions. Sophisticated people today call him naive, crude, and downright rude in his caricature of paganism. But as far as Isaiah was concerned the gods that people made could neither interpret the past nor be prepared for the future. They could not do anything good or help people. They could not do anything bad to harm them either. He painted ironic pictures of people making a god and fixing it with chains and nails so that 'it cannot be moved'. He described the man who chops down a tree and uses part of it as fire-wood and part of it to make a god. To Isaiah the tragic irony of it all was that the pagan could not see that he was deluded in expecting to get help from a piece of wood he had fashioned with his own hands.

It was reported on the news today that the Argentine Government had issued its soldiers with magic crosses to wear, which are reputed to give special protection. Isaiah comments, 'a deluded mind has led him astray, and he cannot deliver himself or say, "Is there not a lie in my right hand?"' (Isaiah 44.20).

This is the tragedy of other religions (and I include every distortion of Christianity under

that heading). They do not lead to salvation.
This is why God is so intolerant. If you want
folk to take the remedy that works, then you
will warn them of cheap imitations that only
do harm.

As I have said, it is fashionable these days
to talk in terms of all the things that we have
in common with those who are not Christians.
We focus on the things in other religions that
agree with Christianity. That may be useful as
a way in to talk to these folk about Christ.
When Paul began with 'the unknown God'
when he was preaching to the Athenians, it
was the way in for evangelism, not an excuse
for a flabby mutual acceptance of one
another's religion as 'just as good'.

The New Testament tells us not to be
mismated with unbelievers. The reasons it
gives are very telling. 'For what partnership
have righteousness and iniquity? Or what
fellowship has light with darkness? What
accord has Christ with Belial? Or what has a
believer in common with an unbeliever? What
agreement has the temple of God with idols?
For we are the temple of the living God' (2
Corinthians 6.14-16). According to that, the
non-Christian is still in bondage to sin, in
darkness, under the Devil and bound up with
idolatry (or man-made gods). God wants
families that will demonstrate both the truth
of the Gospel and the fact that it works. That
is why He has gone on record throughout
Scripture as being fiercely opposed to the

children of God marrying unbelievers. So you
had better make sure that you end up
marrying someone who shares your
commitment to love the Lord and to follow
the teaching of the Bible all the way!

So let's have no more of this nonsense
about trying to help Muslims to be better
Muslims. If Christianity is the truth, then
Muslims have got it wrong. And if they have
got it wrong, then their religion doesn't work.
It does not bring them as sinners into a right
relationship with our terribly holy God. They
need to be converted. That is complicated and
it is hard to put it over in a way that sounds
both loving and respectful. But it is our
responsibility to do it if we would honour
Jesus and care for lost people.

I do hope the Bible study went well. I'm so
glad you believe in preparation these days.
Aim to prepare questions that will make them
all look at their Bibles — and then work out
what it means for us now. Something should
happen after every Bible study. After all, the
Bible has been given to change what we think
and what we do. Resist the temptation to give
all the answers. You might have to wait a bit
for them really to start thinking — but it's
worth it if you can help others to discover for
themselves what the Bible says today.

Now I must go and cram too. I've just been
given four impossible titles for addresses at a
missionary conference, and haven't a clue.
This week has been full of extra crises that eat

up the time — a chap whose fiancée went off
with the Mormons, a missionary with a
mucked up passport, a lass with a missionary
call . . . perhaps? a couple with marriage
plans in chaos, some urgent problem at the
Chinese Fellowship, a colleague rushed off for
emergency surgery, stand-in lectures at the
Bible Training Institute . . . Help! You are
lucky to get this letter . . . Pray for angels to
guard the door and the telephone while this
preparation gets done. That's an *URGENT*
request.

   Rose joins in sending our love.
   DICK.

4

CAN PEOPLE WHO'VE NEVER HEARD BE SAVED?

Dear Dick,

I want to say again that the idea that those who have never heard are lost is much too sweeping and, dare I say it, pretty unbiblical. After all, God saved multitudes of people during Old Testament days — and we can hardly say that they heard the Gospel of Jesus Christ. Granted they had all sorts of hints and promises from the prophets, but they weren't Christians. And they were saved.

I do not pretend to be an expert on how they were saved, but it would seem to me that it was because they turned to God in repentance, offered sacrifice, and threw themselves upon God's mercy. Since Christ's sacrifice on Calvary was 'once and for all', they were obviously saved because of what Jesus had achieved on the cross. But they didn't know about it. There is, after all, little evidence to suggest that Psalm 22 and Isaiah 53 were interpreted in terms of crucifixion until after the event.

Now, if Old Testament Jews were saved because of what Christ did although they had never heard of Him, is it not reasonable to

*argue that the true followers of some other
religions might similarly cast themselves on the
mercy of God in repentance and groping faith,
and be saved by Jesus even though they had
never heard of Him? That would not be saying
that there was some merit in their particular
religion, nor that they had saved themselves.
After all, I can't believe that anyone could seek
after God unless the Spirit of God was already
at work in his heart.*

*I'm sure this is not an heretical idea.
Professor Anderson says: 'Does it not mean
that the man who realizes something of his
sinful need, and throws himself on the mercy
of God with a sincerity which shows itself in
his life (which would always, of course, be a
sure sign of the inward prompting of God's
Spirit, and especially so in the case of one who
had never heard the Gospel), would find that
mercy — although without understanding it —
at the cross on which Christ "died for all"?'[1]
And G Campbell Morgan speaks of 'the glad
and glorious surprise' of finding in Heaven
those who have 'walked in the light they had,
and wrought righteousness and were acceptable
to Him; not because of their morality but by
the infinite merit of the cross.'[2]*

*It's not just biblical scholars who argue this
way, either. It seems to me that Peter said
exactly the same thing to the Italian centurion,*

[1] *Christianity and Comparative Religion* (J N D
   Anderson) page 102.
[2] *The Acts of the Apostles*, page 220.

Cornelius, when he stated, 'in every nation anyone who fears God and does what is right is acceptable to Him' (Acts 10.35).

What I am trying to say is this: I am sure that there will be godly Hindus, Buddhists and Muslims who will wake up in Heaven surprised to find that they are saved through Christ. I cannot bring myself to condemn so many devout and lovely people. And I do not believe that God will condemn them either. The grace of God is bigger than that!

I'm not trying to escape the responsibility to evangelize. But I do think that we need to have much more respect for other people's religions.

Also we must take seriously the news from places like Timor in Indonesia of people being converted by the ministry of angels and the like. Surely that confirms my claim that God can and does save people who have never been evangelized?

I sat next to a Malay on the bus today. Since the days when our imperialistic forefathers did a deal with the sultans, it has been illegal to share the Gospel with a Malay in Malaysia. What hope have they got if your thinking is right?

By the way, I do think you are very right about the need to marry a Christian girl. Fortunately there are plenty of super ones in the YPF here. We'd better have a chat about guidance some time! There is one who really turns me on — hope she is the one in God's plan for me!

Last week's Bible study went really well. It was great to see Ian beginning to understand his need to be a Christian. Do pray for him.
   Take care,
   PAUL.

Dear Paul,
   Thank you for your letter. You have certainly mustered some formidable evidence against me. But I confess that I am still far from being persuaded.
   Perhaps we can begin with Cornelius. Acts 10 is one of my favourite chapters, telling as it does the story of an extremely unwilling missionary being forced to reach out to a wonderfully prepared convert. There is no doubt that God had begun to work in the heart of Cornelius. The biblical narrative tells us that he was a 'devout man who feared God with all his household, gave alms liberally to the people, and prayed constantly to God.' He was deeply religious, a serious seeker. But the narrative will not allow us to say that he was saved. If he had been saved then God would not have had to work so hard to find a missionary to reach him. And we are told that it was only after he had heard the Gospel that he was granted repentance and faith (Acts 11.17-18). Whatever we may say about people

before Christ — and we shall come to that later — we cannot say that this adherent of another religion (Judaism) was saved by his devotion within that religious framework. He had to hear of Jesus. And for all the ministry of angels in the story, a human messenger was required.

Now Peter was chosen to be the missionary for this particular job, and he was certainly not the most likely person to fulfil such a ministry. Cornelius to him was an imperialist and a fascist (although he probably would not have expressed it in those terms!). Cornelius was, after all, involved in the business of keeping the Jews, and others, under the Roman yoke. Moreover Cornelius was a Gentile. And Peter would have been trained from his childhood to thank God daily that he was not one of those. His concept of those who could be saved did not extend beyond his own race.

But God, whose very election of the Jews in the Old Testament had been so that the *nations* could be blessed (Genesis 12.3), is not racially partial. He wants to save people from the nations. And this was the point that Peter grasped and eventually expressed to Cornelius when he said, 'Truly I perceive that God shows no partiality, but in every nation any one who fears him and does what is right is acceptable to him.' He was not saying that he had suddenly discovered that people all over the world could come to God in their own

particular way through their own particular
religions. If that was what he believed, he
would not have gone on to preach the Gospel
to Cornelius. No, what he was saying was that
people of any nationality may come to God if
they come in the right way. That right way is
expressed beautifully at the end of Peter's
sermon when he said that 'everyone who
believes in him (Jesus) receives forgiveness of
sins through his name.' The discovery Peter
made was that belief in Jesus is the
international way of salvation.

In fact, Peter had long known this. He had
expressed it to the religious leaders of his own
people when he was on trial before them
when he said: 'There is salvation in no one
else, for there is no other name under Heaven
given among men by which we must be
saved.' He knew that the devout religious
leaders of his own society needed Christ to
save them. Their deep religious commitment
was not enough. But though he stated this to
them as a universal, 'no other name under
Heaven given among men', he did not really
seem to believe it in his heart in that way. It
was only when he realized that God was
sending angels to prepare foreigners to
respond to the Gospel that he grasped this
truth at gut level. I mean, it hit him so that he
did something about it!

For all the rumours doing the rounds about
Timor, such verifiable evidence as there is
seems to point to angels sometimes preparing

people for the Gospel, but not to them doing the work of an evangelist or missionary. Some years ago on the island of Mindoro in the Philippines, two families among the Tadyawan tribe had the same dream. In it they saw a man in dazzling white who told them that their seeking after God would soon find an answer. The man warned them that someone would arrive in the mountains with the wrong answer, and that after him others would come who had the truth. Some time later a man arrived in their village teaching an idolatrous perversion of the Gospel. On the basis of the dream they sent him packing! Shortly afterwards, two single ladies from our Mission arrived. (Why do we men so often leave the girls to take the gospel to the really tough jungle places?) They were welcomed with open arms and those particular families speedily responded to the Gospel.[1] Like Cornelius, they had been supernaturally prepared for the coming of the Gospel.

But we can't pass the buck to the angels! God willed in both cases to work through His missionaries. That is the way that He will work. We argue at our peril — and at other people's peril too.

Paul, your argument from the Old Testament is an important one. Men like Noah and Abraham were justified by faith. The Old Testament teaches it and the New

[1] This story is told in *Broken Snare* by Caroline Stickley, published by OMF Books.

Testament confirms it. Jesus said that
Abraham 'rejoiced to see his day', but he
certainly was not visited by a missionary
during his pagan days in Ur of the Chaldeans.
He was saved without hearing the Gospel in
its fullness. And he was saved by Christ.

But the fact is that we are not today living
in the time before Christ came. Paul told the
Greeks of Athens, 'The times of ignorance
God overlooked, but now he commands all
men everywhere to repent, because he has
fixed a day on which he will judge the world
in righteousness by a man whom he has
appointed, and of this he has given assurance
to all men by raising him from the dead' (Acts
17.30-31). In other words, whatever we may
have said about the time before Christ, *NOW*
it is not the same. The apostle was quite clear
that the present need is for 'all men
everywhere' to be presented with the urgent
command to repent and trust the risen
Saviour. So it is not surprising that there is
not the remotest hint in the New Testament
of any way that people might be saved
without personally putting their trust in Jesus
and Him alone.

Even if we were to agree with such godly
men as Professor Anderson and Campbell
Morgan, whom I greatly respect, we would
not be left with a great deal of comfort. When
Noah 'found grace in the sight of the Lord',
only seven other people were similarly saved.
The whole of the rest of humanity was

destroyed. When Lot and his two daughters were rescued, the entire population of two cities was destroyed in terrible judgment. In other words, the average pagan is not really a born-again saint without knowing it. The average pagan is a fearfully lost sinner.

Of course, the agony of this is when you translate it into real people. It's easy to talk about the theory, but I find it hard when I think of my Libyan neighbours, knowing that there are virtually no known Libyan Christians today. We would be callous in the extreme if we did not long to find some way whereby some of them at least could be saved.

But the biblical way to achieve this is not to look for hints in Scripture to encourage our wishful thinking. Rather, it is by the loving and costly friendship and evangelism of committed Christians that Libyans will be won. Special pleading can dull our sense of responsibility for such nations, but true realism will seek ways to commend Christ in these so-called closed countries, adopting the apostle's motto that by all means we might save some.

I'm glad you met that Malay fellow. I got to know one on a train from Southampton a while back. He was planning to join the *dakwa* movement on his return to Kuala Lumpur — that's the group which wants to turn Malaysia into another 'Iran under the Ayatollah'. He'd been three years in Britain

— and no one had ever talked to him of Jesus. And he was in a college with a large CU! We can hardly blame our forefathers for their deals with Islam if we do not seek to make amends by giving Muslims the chance to hear the Gospel when they come here.

I'll be praying for Ian and hope for good news in one of your letters soon. Perhaps you might also pray that the Lord will soon open the doors to the Gospel that we closed in Malaysia.

Every blessing,
DICK.

5

A FAIR STANDARD OF JUDGMENT

Dear Dick,

I am sorry, but even after your last thought-provoking letter I am still tremendously perturbed about this business of the unevangelized being condemned. It seems to me ridiculous to suggest that God would condemn people for rejecting the Saviour of whom they have never heard. As Abraham said, 'Shall not the judge of all the earth do right?' Anybody can see that it is not right to condemn the ignorant. If you beat your son Andrew for not fetching your shoes when you did not even ask him, he would have good reason to feel hard done by. God is a better Father than you, not a poor imitation. So I'm sure that the unevangelized will not be condemned. It just wouldn't be fair.

As usual, I'm afraid this is a rushed letter. I've got exams in two days and am cramming like mad. At this rate I'll have shares in Nescafé — the amount I am drinking to keep me awake for study! Anyway, only five more days of trauma and then it will all be over for a while. The Lord has given tremendous

peace. Please pray it will stay that way.
  Yours aye,
  PAUL.

Dear Paul,
  Be prepared for a long letter. Perhaps
you'd better put it on one side until you've
recovered from those exams!
  Whoever suggested that God was going to
condemn people for rejecting someone
they've never heard of? That certainly isn't
the teaching of Scripture. God does not
condemn the man who has not heard as
though he had heard. But the Scripture does
teach that every man stands condemned
before God, and that nobody can argue it's
not fair (Romans 3.19).
  Now I'm not trying to pretend that there
aren't some areas of God's dealings with
people that do seem to be pretty unfair from
our worm's eye view. When faced with such
problems, we have to take seriously Paul's
blunt questions: 'Who are you, a man, to
answer back to God? Will what is moulded
say to its moulder, "why have you made me
thus?" . . .' (Romans 9.20). There are areas
where we have to shut our mouths in humble,
if bewildered, submission. We are not God's
judge. He is the absolute standard of what is

fair and just. Our standards are pretty messy when held up against Him. His standards are not suspect when held up against us!

But God has told us in Scripture that His way of judging those who have never heard is transparently fair. The first sixteen verses of Romans chapter 2 are all about this.

God's Word states that everyone is guilty before Him, firstly because we *have no excuse when judged by our own standards*. Wherever you go in the world people criticize one another. If someone hurts them they react to it. They say, 'You shouldn't have done that'. Maybe they take retaliatory action. When we criticize people we show that we know that particular thing is wrong.

The strange thing about people is that the things they are most keen to criticize in others are the things that they actually do themselves. I was once talking with a militant Communist propagandist in the Philippines, who came from a quite comfortably-off home. She was lambasting the President's wife at great length for the way that she exploited people. After this had gone on for some time I turned and asked the girl if she had a servant in her home — I knew she would have, because almost every home had some poorer person working for them in those days. 'Which is her day off?' I asked. She blushed, embarrassed. She had criticized others so fiercely for exploiting people, but my simple question revealed that she was also exploiting someone else. She stood condemned by her own criticism. And she knew it. I didn't have to say anything more. There was no way she could argue that my gentle question was unfair.

God says that He judges people by the standards they themselves use in criticizing others. That is fair. The trouble is, it is also damning.

The second standard by which God judges the unevangelized is *the standard of their own humanness*. Paul wrote, 'When Gentiles who have not the law (that is the Bible) do by nature what the law requires, they are a law to themselves, even though they do not have the law. They show that what the law requires is written on their hearts . . .' (Romans 2.14,15).

Nobody is suggesting here that pagan people live up to all the standards of God as revealed in the Bible. One would have to be totally ignorant of human nature to suggest such a thing! But when you find pagans who, for example, uphold marriage, or condemn murder, or encourage truth-speaking or the like, they demonstrate that God's standards are not arbitrary but that they fit exactly with the way we are made.

Because this is so, we may rightly expect to find pagans seeing and accepting the reasonableness of such principles. Indeed, they may look at the way that they have worked best and lay down such principles for themselves, without ever knowing what God has said in His Word. For example, I am told that in the early days of the Russian Revolution the people were ordered to work a ten-day week. Efficiency dropped, and it was discovered that people were most productive when they worked six days on and one day off. They did not learn that from the Ten Commandments. But their study of man demonstrated that God's law was right after all! Karl Marx taught that marriage is a bourgeois institution. So in the early revolutionary days the principles of marriage were abandoned. But they discovered that society began to fall apart. People function best in society when principles of marriage are upheld. And that is just what God's Word says!

So it is that those who do not have the Bible are not judged by some arbitrary law of God. Rather they are judged by principles which are self-evident because of the very nature of man. Because of their fallen and twisted nature, they obviously do not arrive at the 'whole counsel of God' just by thinking about it. But then God does not judge them according to this standard either.

It is interesting to compare the judgments that Amos declared in chapters 1 and 2 of his prophecy. The standards by which God judged Israel and Judah (who had the Bible) were higher than those by which He judged the surrounding nations. The pagans were

judged by what we might call universal
standards of human decency. They had done
things that no one could do without a guilty
conscience. So they stood condemned.

And no one can say that such a judgment is
unfair.

The third standard by which God judges
those who have never heard, is the *standard
of their own consciences*. Romans 2.15 says,
'their conscience also bears witness and their
conflicting thoughts accuse or perhaps excuse
them on that day when . . . God judges the
secrets of men by Christ Jesus.' Everyone has
the warning light of conscience. I once saw a
film about a man who didn't. But that was
fiction, not fact! God says that when He
judges pagans their consciences either accuse
them or make excuses. This means that when
certain accusations are brought against them
their consciences agree that that's right. In
other situations their consciences would not
agree and would seek to make excuses. God
is not saying that some pagans would be
excused while others stood condemned, but
that on some sins conscience will agree while
in other areas it would argue against the
accusation.

No one would sensibly want to argue that
conscience is an absolute standard. It is well
known that consciences can be educated, and
also that they can be silenced or pretty much
deadened. Paul warned Timothy of people
who taught what he called the teachings of

demons. He described them as 'hypocritical liars, whose consciences have been seared as with a hot iron' (1 Timothy 4.2, NIV).

So conscience is not an absolute standard, but it is a fair standard. It is not unreasonable to ask people to live according to the warning light that they have built into them.

Now it is on the basis of all this that the apostle argues that the whole world can be held accountable to God, without being able to argue that it's not fair. 'Every mouth may be stopped' (Romans 3.19) — that is, when we get to stand before God neither you nor anyone else in the whole of the world will be able to say that God's condemnation is unfair.

How right you are to affirm so categorically what Abraham said when pleading for Sodom and Gomorrah, 'Shall not the Judge of all the earth do right?' (Genesis 18.25). And so often when we do not know where people stand, it is of tremendous importance and indeed proper comfort to us to turn to such a text. But in all honesty, if you read it in its context, it does not give you the degree of comfort that you are after. You see, God as Judge did what was right for Sodom and Gomorrah. And only one man and two women were saved. Apart from them, the entire population of those two cities was terribly destroyed by our God. This teaches us that when the Judge of all the earth does what is right it is terrifying.

Granted, there was considerable and

horrible evil in those two cities, but then they can hardly be said to have been thoroughly evangelized. All the evidence points to the fact that the witness of Lot and his family was pretty minimal. The pressures of their pagan environment had been allowed to squeeze them into a mould that was not radically different from that of their unsaved neighbours.

If God did what was right for Sodom and Gomorrah, then the unevangelized parts of the world today are in great danger.

Jesus taught that the horror of fire and sulphur that rained down on Sodom would be the same sort of thing that would be happening 'on the day when the Son of Man is revealed' (Luke 17.29-30). This is developed in a dreadful way in the book of Revelation. There we are taught 'the devil who had deceived them was thrown into the lake of fire and sulphur where the beast and false prophet were, and they will be tormented day and night for ever and ever . . . and if anyone's name was not found written in the book of life, he was thrown into the lake of fire' (Revelation 20.10,15). The horror of the Genesis story was a temporary one. The horror of the vision in Revelation is of unending torment 'for ever and ever.'

Have you ever read how John Wesley spoke of his willingness to travel anywhere to present the Gospel to people who were lost? In March 1748 he wrote, 'In plain terms, wherever I see one or a thousand men running into Hell, be it in England, Ireland, or France, yea, in Europe, Asia, Africa, or America, I will stop them if I can: as a minister of Christ, I will beseech them in His name to turn back and be reconciled to God. Were I to do otherwise, were I to let any soul drop into the pit whom I might have saved from everlasting burnings, I am not satisfied that God would accept my plea "Lord, he was not of my parish".[1]

When criticized for preaching in the open air to people who would never have come into church, he commented, 'Now would you really have desired that these poor wretches should have sinned on until they had dropped into Hell? Surely you would not. But by what other means was it possible they should have been plucked out of the fire?' Wesley's convictions about the horror of judgment led him to daring innovations in the work of reaching the lost for Christ. We would do well to follow his example! He was concerned for the whole person — but he didn't let his evangelism get swallowed up in political and social action as so many do today. Salvation was then and still is mankind's No. 1 need.

I began by saying that those who have never heard will not be judged as though they have heard. And I think that I have demonstrated that to be true. But that raises

[1] Letters Vol. II page 137

another consideration. How does God regard
those who do not tell the Gospel to those who
have never heard? He regards them in the
same category as murderers.

When God sent Ezekiel to pass on His
Word to the house of Israel he gave him a
stern warning lest he should back down on the
commission. 'If I say to the wicked, "you shall
surely die", and you give him no warning, nor
speak to warn the wicked from his wicked
way, in order to save his life, that wicked man
shall die in his iniquity; but his blood I will
require at your hand' (Ezekiel 3.18).

God makes it clear here that the
unevangelized do not die because they are
unevangelized but because of their sin. For all
that, He warns that the messenger who keeps
the message to himself is like a murderer in
His sight. So important was this principle that
God repeated it to Ezekiel later in his
ministry (Ezekiel 33.7,8). Today we, who are
the church of Jesus Christ, are answerable for
the unevangelized of the world. Together we
have been given the responsibility to go into
all the world to share the Gospel. And the
church of Jesus Christ is corporately as a
murderer before God. No wonder blessing is
delayed in so many places. Most churches I
preach in here in Scotland have not sent out a
missionary within living memory. How can we
expect blessing in the light of that?

On the individual level the crucial question
we need to answer is 'To whom am *I* sent?'

We are not individually responsible for taking the Gospel to the whole world. We are individually called to witness to particular people in a particular place. Are you fulfilling your responsibility in this respect? Jude encouraged his readers to 'Save some by snatching them out of the fire' (Jude 23). John Calvin commented on this verse, 'When there is a danger of fire, we hesitate not to snatch away violently whom we desire to save; for it would not be enough to beckon with the finger, or kindly to stretch forth the hand.' We need to recover that sense of urgency. We need to face our solemn responsibility.

The unevangelized are judged fairly. They are lost. And the preaching of the Gospel is still their only hope. May God give you the courage to go where you are sent.

Rose and I have to face the same challenge. We cannot hide behind our eight years in the Philippines. That is ancient history now. It was much less of an upheaval to go when we were an engaged couple. Now it would be too easy to argue that the security of the children is more important than the needs of the lost. When I'm honest I have to face the fact that often arguments about children's security can be a cover up for our own selfishness or cowardice. The children are more persistent than us in praying that the Lord will send us back to Asia. Let's pray for each other, that we will not chicken out of what God calls us to dare to do — with Him!

Rose joins me in sending our love in Christ.
We are keen to know your results.
Every blessing
DICK.

6

WHAT PEOPLE REALLY NEED

Dear Dick,

Your ideas of Hell are hopelessly out of date. They belong to previous centuries, not today. Maybe Wesley used graphic ideas about Hell to scare people into becoming Christians. But it seems to me that such ideas were either dug up out of the Old Testament or were in fact not biblical at all. Visions of Hell are the sort of thing one thinks of when one looks at medieval works of art with all sorts of skinny nudes being hurled into a flaming pit. They imagined horned demons prodding with pitchforks, and people subjected to every sort of torture.

Frankly, I can't understand how such ideas managed to stick with the church after Jesus had come. He, after all, taught that God SO LOVED the world. He showed that God was loving, kind, gentle, and even full of fun. That is what appeals to modern man.

Nobody in his right mind would talk about Hell from a pulpit these days. You'd certainly get labelled as a melodramatic Victorian if you tried it at an evangelistic crusade. As far as people of today are concerned, it is this life that matters. People don't become Christians out of fear of Hell. And you won't persuade anyone to become a missionary because of the problem of Hell either.

Surely we must get back to the gentle and gracious teaching of Jesus and leave Hell to the Old Testament and the Middle Ages.

Did you see that television documentary about the horrors the Khmer experienced during Pol Pot's régime? Imagine folk being buried up to their necks and left to die, family life almost totally destroyed, and the ache of famine and fear of death on every side. The love of Jesus in my heart cried out for justice.

How can you be so negative about Christian political and social action? The Khmer need political rights, a just society, food and clothing. They certainly do not need to be confronted with an extra fear — of Hell. They need love.

By the way, I got through the exam. Thanks for your prayers,

Your brother,
PAUL.

Dear Paul,

Congratulations on your exam result!

I'm glad that you begin by recognizing the fact that the fear of Hell used profoundly to motivate people. When Hudson Taylor, the founder of our Mission, was only eighteen years old, he wrote to his younger sister, 'I have a stronger desire than ever to go to China. That land is ever in my thoughts. Think of it — 360 million souls, without God or hope in the world! . . . dying . . . without any of the consolations of the Gospel.'

It was the sense of the lostness of the unevangelized Chinese which drove him to begin an amazing pioneer missionary venture. Later in life he wrote, 'I would never have thought of going out to China had I not believed that the Chinese were lost and needed Christ.'

General Booth, who founded the Salvation Army, said he could wish his Christian workers might spend 'one night in Hell' in order to see the urgency of their evangelistic task.

But certainly these days we have changed our vocabulary. We rarely talk of 'being saved'. And Hell is seldom if ever mentioned in the majority of pulpits in our land. And that includes the evangelical ones!

As you say, today we are concerned with the 'now' rather than the 'hereafter'. I recently learnt that one fine University Christian Union's sizeable 'missionary' giving over a period of years was wholly devoted to a social work project in Latin America. The old urgency that people should hear the Gospel and find eternal life has been replaced

by concern for political freedom, for feeding
the hungry and healing the sick.

Now I certainly do not object to these
important concerns. Having worked in the
Philippines during a time of extensive
Communist propaganda and unrest, I could
hardly say that issues of political freedom are
unimportant. They matter immensely to me.
Without that conviction I would never have
won a hearing from the militant Maoists who
frequently attended our meetings there.

Having grappled with problems of
undernourishment and seen first hand the
result of horrific natural disasters, I believe
wholeheartedly in the importance of famine
and disaster relief. So of course I am
committed to the work of organizations like
Tear Fund both in my own Christian giving
and in my concern to encourage suitable
personnel to work with them. A number of
friends of mine are giving themselves to serve
the urgent needs of the Khmer you saw on
television.

And knowing what it is to move out of the
shelter of the National Health Service into
countries where medical care can often work
out more expensive than the life-style at the
top of the Hilton Hotel, I am actively on the
lookout for openings for missionary medicine.
Some of the Filipinos who used to come to
our lay training classes in Manila are now
meeting medical needs in the refugee camps
of Thailand. And that rejoices my heart.

But the fundamental command of Jesus in terms of our world involvement was to go and *MAKE DISCIPLES*, and the reason for this was that the most fundamental need of the nations is to be saved from the horror of Hell and of lostness.

Honestly, I don't know how to communicate this greatest of human needs. You cannot take a picture of a lost and starving soul. The so-called Christians in Laodicea were described by the Saviour as 'wretched, pitiable, poor, blind, and naked' (Revelation 3.17). The trouble is, no photographer could have shown that diagnosis in a moving way to a twentieth-century Christian public.

This was brought home to me graphically recently when I was talking with one of the staff of the National Bible Society of Scotland. A man well qualified in the science of advertising, he was seeking to prepare materials to boost an appeal to the Scottish Christian public for money to provide Bibles for those in the refugee camps along the border of Thailand. The problem he had was that all his photographs of people in the refugee camps made them look reasonably well fed and more or less contented. They would not stir people to generosity.

I pointed out to him that if the photographs had made the people look miserable and starving, then the British public would not send money to provide them with Bibles but

would send it to relief agencies instead with
the pious — and wrong — remark, 'You can't
preach the Gospel to an empty stomach.'
(The Word of God would teach that you can't
JUST preach the Gospel to an empty
stomach). Then his advertising would defeat
its very object. He saw my point, but like me
still had to wrestle with the problem, 'How do
you sell the greatest need of people to a
Christian public that has forgotten the lostness
of the unevangelized?'

You don't even seem to be aware of the
real source of the Bible's teaching on Hell and
lostness! You seem to want to play it off
against the teaching of Jesus, but in fact
almost all the teaching on Hell in Scripture is
from the recorded sayings of Jesus Himself. If
you don't want a doctrine of Hell, you don't
want the teaching of Jesus. If Jesus was wrong
about Hell, then we've no reason to think
with any certainty that He was right about the
things we prefer to believe. But if Jesus was
who He claimed to be — the Son of the
Living God — then He got it right — all of it!

Now I want to take you on a gallop through
the Gospels to see how the horror of Hell is
inescapable if you take the words of Jesus at
all seriously.

The first thing I want you to recognize is
that *the expressed mission of Jesus was to
save people from Hell*.

In the time of Jesus, most people would
have said that if anybody was damned it was

Zacchaeus. As a chief tax-collector he had sided with the pagans and was involved in vicious exploitation at the expense of others. He was regarded as a hopeless case, and the people as a whole were appalled that Jesus should actually want to have fellowship with him; for that was the implication of asking hospitality of the man.

Jesus in one breath silenced the critics and encouraged the new-born faith in this till now evil man. He said, 'The Son of Man came to seek and to save *THE LOST*' (Luke 19.10).

So Jesus defined those for whom He had come as *lost* people.

You will remember that the angel told Joseph that Mary's son was to be called Jesus 'for he will save his people from their sins' (Matt 1.21). So the lostness problem is a problem of sin.

And if the angel's comment seems to have a peculiarly Jewish application, then John 3.16 certainly doesn't. 'For God so loved the world that he gave his only Son, that whoever believes in him should not perish but have eternal life.'

You will remember that you quoted this verse at me to justify your rejection of the doctrine of Hell. In fact the whole verse in context supports it! Jesus came so that people 'should not *perish*'. Look at the next few verses. Jesus' ministry was to rescue folk from the consequences of standing condemned before God. Perhaps some other time I'll

expound the whole chapter to you. But you've
heard me before, and know that brevity is not
my great gift! And I've got to dash this letter
off now between a load of other things. So I'll
just refer you to the last verse of the chapter.
It says, 'He who believes in the Son has
eternal life; he who does not obey the Son
shall not see life, but the wrath of God rests
upon him' (John 3.36).

While this verse clearly teaches that the one
who hears the Gospel and rejects it is in great
peril, it also shows us some pretty unnerving
things about those who have never heard. If
the man who rejects the Gospel does not see
life — or isn't really living — then the same is
at present true of the unevangelized. We are
not told that the man who rejects the Gospel
loses the life that he once had. Rather we are
told that he misses the chance of having it at
all.

When it is said that the wrath of God rests
(or remains) upon the one who rejects the
Gospel, the implication is that the wrath of
God also hangs over the one who has not
heard. For to hear and not receive salvation is
to find that the wrath of God just stays where
it already is, hanging over your head.

In the first part of Romans Paul similarly
argued that all over the world people are in a
present experience of the wrath of God. If
folk are on the wrong side of God in this life,
what have they got to look forward to in the
next? So Jesus came to save from Hell.

The second thing that we need to say is that *the fundamental emphasis of Jesus' mission was salvation*.

There was great need of political emancipation in the time of Christ. When Jesus applied Isaiah 61.1-2 to Himself in His home town synagogue, He claimed that God had anointed Him 'to preach good news to the poor . . . to proclaim release to the captives and recovering of sight to the blind, to set at liberty those who are oppressed' (Luke 4.18). He almost seemed to be taking on a political programme. Indeed, some pseudo-Christian guerilla movements have claimed this text in their favour. But if these words were to be fulfilled in a literal and political sense, then Jesus was the most miserable failure. For example, the only prisoner released by Him was Barabbas — and that cost the Saviour His life in exchange!

Jesus' emphasis wasn't on feeding the hungry either. In three years of ministry, He is recorded as having only twice fed considerable crowds in a miraculous way. But Jesus was greatly alarmed when He felt that some would turn Him into the simple answer to famine relief. He said, 'You seek me, not because you saw signs, but because you ate your fill of the loaves. Do not labour for the food which perishes, but for the food which endures to eternal life, which the Son of Man will give to you; for on him has God the Father set his seal' (John 6.26f). In other

words, His ministry was not to focus attention
on stomachs but on what used to be called
'souls'.

Others have always wanted to make Jesus
an efficient alternative to the aspirin bottle.
When news of His power to heal got around,
people would even rip the roof off to get at
Him. Now Jesus was really concerned about
people's bodies — He even insisted that the
first missionaries that He sent out should 'heal
the sick' (Luke 10.9). It is significant,
however, that when people tried to
monopolize His time for the problems of
sickness and demon possession He left them
behind, telling them, 'I must preach the good
news of the kingdom of God to the other
cities also; for I was sent *for this purpose*'
(Luke 4.43). His healings undoubtedly
demonstrated the love of God for the whole
person. But the priority of His ministry was
the preaching of the Gospel — good news of
salvation.

Isn't this why the Gospels spend so much
time talking about the death of Jesus? What
other biography have you read that similarly
focuses on the last 24 hours of the subject's
life? Jesus' major work was to die. He saved
us on the cross. But that's a meaningless
statement if there's nothing to be saved from.

What I am trying to say is this: Jesus cared
for *whole* people.

Evangelicals used to be accused of caring
for the needs of the soul and ignoring the

needs of the body. To such an approach the Bible speaks clearly, 'If a brother or sister is ill-clad and in lack of daily food, and one of you says to them, "Go in peace, be warmed and filled," without giving them the things needed for the body, what does it profit?' (James 2.15f).

Now the pendulum has swung to the other extreme, and evangelism is left out. We naively deceive ourselves into the modern myth that the Church is established in all the world, and that such evangelism as remains to be done can be safely left to the local churches.

Each of us has to work out how he is going to spend his time. And the Spirit does not make all of us evangelists. But Jesus was clear that His priority was bringing people eternal life. Everything took second place to the preaching of the Gospel, to the sharing of the Good News. Therefore, this must be the Church's priority too.

Of course we must be loving rather than judgmental and threatening. But, if we take Jesus' teaching seriously, we shall want to make people face their most urgent need of the Saviour. It is hardly loving to leave them thinking everything is OK — or that everything would be OK if only they had better hospitals, better homes, better education and better government. If Jesus is right, people are in grave danger. Our message loses its credibility when we have no urgency in evangelism. As someone once put it: 'Either you don't really believe in Hell — or you are culpably callous.'

The apostle Paul wrote: 'Therefore, knowing the fear (terror) of the Lord, we persuade men . . . for the love of Christ controls us (leaves us no choice)' (2 Cor. 5.11,14). The terror of the Lord was no theoretical doctrine to him. Paul had once stood before Christ as an unbeliever; he also knew the love of Christ reaching out from his heart to people of many different nationalities. And yet in one of his circular letters, he asked his friends to pray that he would boldly declare the gospel, 'as I ought to speak' (Ephesians 6.20). Imagine Paul being tempted to chicken out on evangelism! It seems he was. He certainly appreciated that there was supernatural opposition to it (Ephesians 6.12). And the Devil will try to side-track us from evangelism too.

In 1973 Chhirc Taing, who was later martyred for his daring missionary faith, begged me to take time on my furlough to find missionaries for his country of Cambodia. The time was short and the people of Phnom Penh knew it. A country that had never had more than a handful of Christians was suddenly longing to know the Gospel. Friends of mine who visited found even customs officials pulling them on one side in the hope that they might tell them the way to Christ! But the number of missionary recruits was pathetic. I'm sure that Pol Pot will have much to answer for at the judgment seat. Few men in our time have been responsible for such a reign of terror. But I fear more for what we in the Church worldwide will have to answer for. By and large, we left a people crying for help to go to Hell.

Paul, keep up your friendships with the foreign students, and we'll pray for openings to talk about Jesus. Ho Chi Minh once worked in a London hotel. Sadly, he was not reached for Christ while he was here. Who knows what your friends might come to do for God . . . or for the Evil One.

With much love in Christ,
DICK.

7

THE HORROR OF VENGEANCE

Dear Dick,
One of the things that really turns me off
when we get on to this whole subject of
judgment is the vindictiveness of it all. I really
find it terribly disgusting. All this about fire
and brimstone, burning, wrath, and endless
punishment. Much of it seems to me to come
in the writings of the apostle Paul. It seems
that all his experiences of persecution and riots
left their scars on him. He felt some sort of
psychological need to get his own back. So he
writes these dreadful passages depicting Jesus
in flaming fire inflicting vengeance on people.
I find it hard to accept what you said about
Jesus' teaching on Hell. After all, when once
the people in a village would not receive Jesus,
His disciples James and John, who were with
good reason named the 'sons of thunder', said
'Lord do you want us to bid fire come down
from Heaven and consume them?' Jesus, most
significantly, turned and rebuked them (Luke
9.53-55).
Jesus, it seems to me, rejected the blood and
fire approach of Jewish apocalyptic. He is
called the Friend of Sinners, not their

slaughterer.

You are often saying that we need to follow the example of Jesus. If we do that, then we will stop talking about Hell, and trying to frighten people into the Kingdom, teaching them instead that Jesus has rejected such awful ideas and is loving and gracious and accepting towards them.

I went to see 'Chariots of Fire' the other night. It was great to see a film about a Christian with principles, that worked in the secular cinema. Some of my friends were very impressed — especially by the bit about 'God honours those who honour him.' You must go and see it sometime.

God bless you,
PAUL.

Dear Paul,

Thank you for once again coming back at me with some very important comments.

I am so relieved to find you are appalled at the way the apostle Paul describes the vengeance of our God. I often turn to those terrible words he wrote: 'God deems it just to repay with affliction those who afflict you, and to grant rest with us to you who are afflicted, when the Lord Jesus is revealed from Heaven with His mighty angels in

flaming fire, inflicting vengeance upon those
who do not know God and upon those who
do not obey the gospel of our Lord Jesus.
They shall suffer the punishment of eternal
destruction and exclusion from the presence
of the Lord and from the glory of his might,
when he comes on that day . . .' (2 Thess.
1.6-10).

There are few words in Scripture more
designed to set our hair standing on end. I
never cease to be terrified by them. The
picture of our Lord Jesus Christ positively
inflicting vengeance is awful. The way that the
destruction is described as eternal is bad
enough. But when this is amplified to mean
that they shall be forever excluded from the
Lord's presence it seems even worse.

I confess that I find what you would call the
blood and thunder of these verses particularly
agonizing. The fact that such vengeance falls
upon those 'who do not know God' as well as
upon those who 'do not obey the gospel of
our Lord Jesus' is most alarming.

I don't like it, and you don't like it. Shall
we therefore decide that we are not going to
believe it? If we could establish that this was
just the opinion of some vindictive old man,
then we would be justified in throwing it out.
But it isn't — and that is the trouble. It is, I
believe, an honest statement of the truth
about the human predicament. We do need to
be saved from the wrath of God and not just
from our own little problems.

You will know, of course, that my conviction that it is the truth stems principally from my belief that the whole Bible is the Word of God. But even if I did not believe that, I would still have to argue that Paul is not going off on a line of his own by teaching in this way. The recorded sayings of Jesus fit exactly with the horrific statements of Paul.

Take for example the ways in which Jesus Himself described the lostness of those He came to save.

Many religious people at the time of Christ were interested in having religious discussions about Him. But Jesus cut through their discussion, teaching them that academic detachment was dangerous. They needed to make a personal commitment to Him or they would 'die in their sins' (John 8.24 in context). He clearly regarded this matter of dying still bound up with your sin as a very dangerous predicament. So He was at pains to impress upon people the need to deal with their sin or be in big trouble.

On one occasion people came to Him discussing the problem of what we in the 20th century would call 'innocent victims' of disasters. Some people had been cruelly murdered by the politically ambitious Pontius Pilate. Others had been sadly crushed to death when a tower had collapsed. The people at the time of Christ did not talk glibly of innocent victims, but rather assumed such tragedies were a sure indication that those

killed were guilty of secret sins. Jesus
corrected this mistaken idea but at the same
time took the opportunity to impress on the
people the need to deal with sin. He said,
'Unless you repent you will all likewise perish'
(Luke 13.1-5).

News has recently reached us of a tragic
plane crash in the USA. Many died a horrible
death, some drowning in icy water. They were
no worse sinners than the rest of us. But
undoubtedly many of them died without
knowing anything of the power of Jesus to
deal completely with the sin problem. They
'died in their sins'. Jesus today would again
impress upon us the importance of recognizing
the serious danger of *those still alive* who have
not had their sin dealt with.

On another occasion Jesus looked at the
very meticulous religious observance of the
Scribes and Pharisees. These people had
developed a form of religion that would
impress many, with its high standards of
commitment and the huge sacrifices involved.
They were committed to a form of evangelism
too, bringing many others to this same
wholehearted standard of commitment. But it
was manmade religion, a way of self-salvation.
Jesus fiercely referred to those who practise
it, and to their converts, as 'children of Hell'
(see Matthew 23.15 etc). We who are children
of God belong with God. Those who are
children of Hell belong there. Clearly that is a
dreadful thing to say. We would certainly

think twice before referring to someone as a
child of Hell, or as a child of the Devil. We
have no business to speak like that. But Jesus
does, and did!

Now God, according to Jesus, did not
'design' Hell for people. God's heart has
always been set on bringing people to
Himself. Nonetheless, Jesus, the Son of Man,
warned that He Himself would say from His
glorious throne, 'Depart from me, you cursed,
into the eternal fire prepared for the Devil
and his angels' (Matthew 25.41). On your
terms, that sounds horribly Pauline. In fact it
is Jesus Himself who says 'Get out' and
consigns people to the horror of Hell-fire.

When one looks further into the teaching of
Jesus, one can hardly escape the fact that He
taught that Hell was an irreversible horror.
The writer of the letter to the Hebrews said,
'It is appointed for men to die once, and after
that comes judgment' (Hebrews 9.27). And
Jesus Himself maintained that death brought
an end to the opportunity of getting right with
God. This is shown most graphically in the
parable of Dives and Lazarus in Luke 16. In
the parable Jesus told of an affluent man who
died, and in the place of the dead was
tormented and in 'anguish in this flame'. He
also told of a poor beggar, Lazarus, who on
dying joined the bliss of the people of God.
The parable does not tell us the grounds on
which either man was assigned to his
particular destination. However, the rich man

realized that unless the members of his family repented of their sin they would end up as he did, which implies that no one is in Heaven unless his sin has been dealt with. And that is consistent with the rest of the teaching of Scripture.

Jesus did, however, go into alarming detail in this parable about the state of the lost man. He explained that between the lost and the saved 'a great chasm has been fixed, in order that those who would pass from here to you may not be able, and none may cross from there to us.' Such comment from Jesus would be pointless unless He had wanted His listeners to understand quite clearly that there was no second chance after death. There is no concept of serving time in Hell before going to Heaven. There is no doctrine of purgatory. Those who die without a Saviour from sin die in their sins and are terribly, irreversibly, *lost*.

We who rejoice in the lovely invitations of Jesus to come to Him, naturally find it hard to conceive of Him ever saying, 'Get out' to anyone. But in fact Jesus tells us that at the . judgment He will most certainly speak in such a way.

In the Sermon on the Mount He said that at that time He would say, 'I never knew you; depart from me, you evil doers'. This was even to be said to people who called Him Lord without in fact having a personal, life-changing relationship with Him (Matthew 7.21-23).

One day, as He was on His way through towns and villages, teaching, He was asked about those who would be saved. Again He said that there would be those to whom He would solemnly say, 'I tell you, I do not know where you come from; depart from me, all you workers of iniquity!' And He warned them that when He said, 'Get out' in this way they would be consigned to 'weep and gnash their teeth' (Luke 13.27,28). The sheer terror of it is this time shown in the awful grief and remorse that those punished in this way would feel.

It was, I think, Amy Carmichael who one night had a horrific vision or dream of humanity walking to a cliff edge and one by one dropping over to a terrible death. But, frankly, this vision was not original to Amy Carmichael. It was such a vision that profoundly motivated Jesus. And once more He sought to pass it on to His disciples, that they might similarly be gripped with the urgency of the situation. He said to them, 'The gate is wide and the way is easy, that leads to destruction, and those who enter by it are many' (Matthew 7.13). Jesus saw humanity rushing along a massive motorway towards a disastrous precipice. He did not see Hell as the designation of a handful of Hitlers and the like. In this nightmare picture He describes those going that way as 'many'.

Perhaps the most graphic and in a way disgusting word Jesus used to convey His

concept of Hell was the word Gehenna.
Gehenna was the rubbish tip outside
Jerusalem. There was always rubbish burning
there and always a stinking mess for the
worms to get fat on. Jesus spoke of God
consigning people to the rubbish tip. The
picture is utterly revolting; one of people
being thrown into Hell, 'where their worm
does not die, and the fire is not quenched'
(Mark 9.47-48). But rather than telling people
not to believe it, He urged them that any
sacrifice was worth making (even physical
amputation!) in order to avoid it.

This same picture is to be found in one of
the very rare Old Testament references to
Hell. The last verse of Isaiah's prophecy
speaks of the lost being where 'their worm
shall not die, their fire shall not be quenched,
and they shall be an abhorrence to all flesh'
(Isaiah 66.24). But that chapter too is one in
which God spoke of His plan to come and
gather all nations and tongues to Himself.
Because God believes in Hell, He believes in
mission. Because Jesus believed in Hell, He
came to save.

There are many parts of the world where it
is very dangerous to become a Christian.
Some years ago the Indonesian evangelist
Octavianus conducted a campaign among the
Muslims of South Thailand. I'm told he
warned them that if they came to Christ they
might well have to die for it. Nonetheless, he
urged them to come to Christ. That is

consistent with the teaching of Jesus. It is better to be killed for being a Christian than to die without Christ. Jesus put it this way, 'I tell you, my friends, do not fear those who kill the body, and after that have no more that they can do. But I will warn you whom to fear: fear him who, after he has killed, has power to cast into Hell; yes, I tell you, fear him!' (Luke 12.4-5). 'They can only kill you', said Jesus to those who thought it might be too costly to become Christians. The murdered Christian goes to be with Christ.

This was very strikingly brought home to me when a dear friend of ours was murdered in Manila. Moody was the leader of the lively Christian Union at a university where the Muslim fraternities made covenants that they would murder any of their number who became a Christian. But his death was not a matter of religious persecution. He was shot on a bus for his watch. Nonetheless, I don't think that it was being super-spiritual to see the hand of Satan in this tragic event.

That very morning Moody had been reading Romans 8 in his quiet time. When he got to the final verses of the chapter he became so excited that he actually shouted them out — 'For I am sure that neither death . . . nor anything else in all creation, will be able to separate us from the love of God in Christ Jesus our Lord.' The other lads in the dormitory were awakened rather rudely to these wonderful assurances. That evening they knew the reason why.

So Jesus said to His friends that when people had killed them, that was all they could do, because death does not separate the believer from His Saviour. But if that is true, we need to face the warning that goes alongside the promise. We need to fear the one who has the power to cast into Hell.

So often people do not become Christians because they're afraid of what will happen to them if they do. And Jesus never suggested that those who followed Him would not have problems. Rather, He warned that they might well have a pretty rough time of it. But He was determined that those counting the cost should consider the alternative to conversion very seriously.

On one occasion, talking to a curious but uncommitted crowd, Jesus warned them that He was not interested in cheap discipleship. They had to count the cost of following Him and do it properly or not at all. But He went on to warn them that they should also count the cost of trying to fight against God. When you realize that the enemy you are taking on is bound to win in the end, you make every effort to secure terms of peace (Luke 14.28-32).

A rubbish tip is a horrific place for a person to end up, one to be avoided at all costs. And the expressed mission of Jesus was to save people from such a horrendous destination. But this rubbish tip concept of Hell conveys

another idea which is equally tragic. It means
that God regards those whom He consigns
there as rubbish. And that is how He thinks
of wasted lives, lives that have not been
according to the Divine pattern, lives that
have not submitted to God's will or God's
way, sinful lives, godless lives.

Rubbish!

There is no doubt that God has set the
highest value on reclaiming rubbishy lives. He
set the value of the life of His only Son
against the value of every lost person who will
ever be saved. So we must never imply that
God casually writes people off. He doesn't.
Remember John 3.16? 'For God so loved the
world that he gave his only Son, that whoever
believes in him should not perish but have
eternal life'.

Jesus is certainly not vindictive. Like the
Father in Heaven He takes no pleasure in the
death of the wicked. That was why He so
firmly rebuked the Sons of Thunder for their
longing to witness the fire of God. But that
does not mean that He pretended Hell was
not there or refused to talk about it.

He was honest about it. He warned about
it. He spoke with graphic horror about it.
You may object to the very idea of
frightening people into the Kingdom, and it's
true that fear may not be the best of motives
for coming to Christ. But then, who ever has
come to Christ with other than sinful mixed-
up motives? Fear is a perfectly valid incentive

to respond to Christ. People are in danger.
People are lost. They are Hell-bound.

My children think they can swim quite well.
In fact, the boys are not yet very competent.
But they are quite proud of their present
achievements. I can imagine one of them in
the middle of the river confidently shouting
'Leave me alone, I can swim well enough to
get to the side'. He can't. I might tell him,
'Grab the lifebelt or you'll drown!' That is the
truth of the matter, and because of his
misguided self-confidence he may need to be
shaken by that fearful statement to recognize
that he cannot rescue himself.

Jesus was not afraid to warn of danger. His
preaching made people sit up and think!

Too often in our evangelism today the
message seems to be that Jesus is the spiritual
aspirin for any type of spiritual or emotional
headache you may happen to feel. It is hardly
surprising that this effeminate Gospel has
failed to build a manly church. The God of
the Bible is tough, holy, and desperately
dangerous, as well as being loving and
compassionate. It is the whole vision of our
God that breaks and remakes people. So we
must not simply communicate the 'nice bits',
or people get the wrong idea altogether and
think that they can play around with God
Himself.

A sense of the horror of Hell will not only
mould our message, it will also profoundly
motivate us to mission. When Jude described

evangelism as 'snatching people out of the fire' he showed how urgent it really is.

My school used to have its own Christian Union Camp, at which I was converted. The year I went to University two other boys were converted at that Camp. One of them died a week later, falling from a cliff; the other was killed in a cycling accident about a month later. A young medical missionary who was present at that camp commented afterwards, 'We so often think that this camp is strategic in preparing boys for Christian ministry, for missionary work, for outreach through many professions and jobs. That is important, but it is not our fundamental role. Our job is to prepare boys for Heaven.'

I believe that if Jesus had not held this conviction of the eternal significance of the Gospel, then He would easily have been side-tracked into other important, but secondary concerns. He would have become preoccupied with health and food, with political freedom and social welfare. But His concern was to bring the Good News of salvation. That is primary, because it is what has eternal significance for the hearers.

If you believe in the fire, then you cannot regard mission as a casual option or an occasional hobby. It is No. 1 priority.

I've just had a new list of our mission's openings for work in East Asia. We have about 350 openings for Bible ministry — many of them for pioneering where there is little or no Christian witness. It would be really great to see a few more men going to take them up, while we've still got the opportunity.

What a long letter. I'm sorry. At least you know that I care to see you convinced.

Sadly I missed 'Chariots of Fire' when it was up here in Glasgow. I noticed that even 'Newsweek' was enthusiastic about it — and they can be pretty cynical. The boys want me to take them when it comes back. They have heard of Eric Liddell at school. But I doubt if our David could sit still through a full-length movie yet!

Every blessing,
DICK.

8

OTHER FAITHS WORK

Dear Dick,
I have had a rather unsettling week.
Following on from the convictions that you
expressed in your recent letter, I have gone out
of my way to try and share my testimony with
some of the foreign students at college.
I began with a Muslim from Saudi Arabia.
He has been friendly for quite some time, but I
have never had the courage to share with him
about my faith. I talked to him of what it
meant to me to have a personal relationship
with God. To my great surprise he told me that
he also had such a relationship, and how it
had made such a difference to him during the
tensions of examinations.
Later I was talking to a Singaporean. I told
him some of the exciting things that the Spirit
of God has been doing during these days. To
my great embarrassment, he told me that
people have been speaking in tongues in his
religion for ages, and that there are also those
who can apparently deal with demon
possession. So the old Chinese religions
evidently work too.
At the same time my girlfriend was

witnessing to a Filipino nurse. She didn't seem to be a real Christian, in our sense of the word, and had lots of images in her room. She showed Rachel a special medallion of St Martin that she keeps for protection. She told her that her mother had been protected by this medal during a dangerous pregnancy, and that her brother had been healed in answer to her prayers to St Martin.

Now in all these cases their religions are clearly not the same as ours. But for all that, they prove and experience the blessing of God. Many who belong to the Hari Krishna group in college speak of the peace that comes over them as they recite the mantra in exactly the same terms that we use to speak of the help that prayer brings. So I have become discouraged in my evangelism. If they have the blessings that the Gospel brings through their religions, then it seems a bit superfluous for me to go and tell them our message instead.

I don't like thinking that way since for myself I know that the Gospel is true. But all the evidence seems to point in that direction.

Your bewildered brother in Christ,
PAUL.

Dear Paul,
I'm sorry you have had such a traumatic

beginning to your missionary endeavour in college. It certainly does come as a bit of a shock to find that other religions work, or at least appear to.

But really, when you stop and think, it's not terribly surprising that we should see things happening in non-Christian religions. Paul, when he was in prison and having a really rough time of it because he was a missionary, wrote to remind the Ephesians that, 'We are not contending against flesh and blood, but against the principalities, against the powers, against the world rulers of this present darkness, against the spiritual hosts of wickedness in the heavenly places' (Ephesians 6.12). That is to say, as far as people and manmade religion is concerned, there are no grounds for expecting these people to have a testimony. But behind it all is a supernatural opposition. And we would be naive in the extreme if we supposed that this opposition could not make things work!

The problem is that when it does work we so often don't know how to proceed. In our culture we no longer ask 'Is it right?' or 'Is it true?' We are merely interested in whether or not it works. And if it works, we reckon it is worth having.

This was alarmingly brought home to me when I was talking with some Christian Union members about a man in Singapore who was demon possessed. When dealt with by the minister of a Bible Presbyterian Church there, this man spoke in tongues, which were recognized as four different languages, none of which the man himself had ever learnt. The man was delivered from the demons by the power of Christ.

To my great amazement one of the students commented, 'But isn't it rather useful to be able to speak four other languages without ever having learnt them?' And he was a committed Christian. You see, he was more interested in the usefulness of the experience than in its origin. It was in fact of the Devil, and devilishly dangerous. But if we don't learn to ask where things come from, then we will be fooled by the testimony that 'it works!'

I often like to think of the Devil as following the same techniques as a good Chinese business man. I observed in Manila that Chinese business men did well because they gave good discounts in order to secure you as a regular customer. They did not aim at big quick profits but rather at securing your commitment to them. Even a small short-term loss is good investment if it secures a long-term profit.

The Devil is happy to give discounts in order to secure regular customers too. So he gives a healing here, a deep religious experience there, speaking in tongues somewhere else, and even the occasional deliverance from a particular evil spirit, in order to secure the person in his present commitment. It is a small discount if it

persuades a person not to transfer his
allegiance to the only Saviour!

The New Testament reminds us that the
Devil frequently disguises himself as an angel
of light. I like the graphic way the cartoonist
for the Good News Bible draws a dazzling
angel with small horns beginning to show. The
Devil's evil has many good points about it. If
it didn't, then only an idiot would be fooled
by it. It is the good points that people notice,
and so they get conned.

When you look at the ways the apostles
preached the Gospel, you will find that most
of what they said Jesus could do is claimed in
some way or another by other religions.
Perhaps we'd do well to look at different
aspects of the Gospel and see this, and try at
the same time to understand why it is that
their claims are unacceptable.

Let's go back to Peter's sermon to
Cornelius and his household, in Acts 10.36-43.

Peter began by impressing upon his listeners
that God Himself has spoken. He has spoken
to Israel in history.

When we ask the question, 'What is God
like and what does He purpose to do with
us?', we really do not know where to begin if
we are left to our own devices. We have
nothing but our own speculation to go on.

Not long ago a book was written by a
selection of well-known people entitled 'The
God that I Want.' But the question is not,
what sort of God do you want, but what sort

of God is there.

The Christian Gospel is that God has revealed Himself, and that revelation is clearly and accurately given in the Bible. I don't really think I need to argue that with you, since I know that you share the same convictions and I can remember the time when those convictions were confirmed in your own experience. Do you remember how you set out to read John's Gospel in order to discover who Jesus really was? You wrote to me, 'It was embarrassing; here was this person making the most outrageous claims, but the staggering thing was, He was making them on my life!' So for you it is not simply a matter of believing the truth of the Bible, but of discovering it in a deeply personal way.

It is the Bible that reveals God to people all over the world. I once met a young man in India who had set himself to seek the true God. In his search he committed himself to worship the snake. Eventually he came to believe he would find the right answers in the Bible, if only he could find a Bible. He couldn't. But one day he read an anti-Christian tract put out by the local temple, which quoted from the Bible. So he became sure that there must be a Bible somewhere in the local temple. When he found it there he began to read at Genesis — hardly the place I would recommend the average seeker to begin! However, he said that he very rapidly came to know this was not just another religious book, but God's Word, and God speaking to him.

A friend of mine once gave a Bible to a hospitalized Hindu scholar he knew. One day as he was visiting him in hospital the scholar asked him if he realized why the Bible was the Word of God. He then went on to explain that all the stories of the Hindu gods in his own sacred writings simply mirrored the personalities, and indeed the vices, of the respective authors. Not so the God of the Bible. And the New Testament writers, so full of quirks, weaknesses and failings, write none of these characteristics back on to the life of the Saviour, Jesus.

It is not a matter of saying the Bible works and therefore it must be true, but rather that the Bible is true and therefore it works.

But the basic Gospel assertion is not, of course, about the reliability of Scripture. It is about the supremacy and glory of Jesus. Peter told Cornelius, 'He is Lord of all'; that is to say, He is out-classed nowhere. So we may borrow a phrase from the advertising world and say 'Beware of imitations'. And of course we need to expect there to be imitations, because the Devil knows how wonderfully attractive Jesus is to people who realize their lostness.

The supremacy of Jesus is claimed in several different areas which are relevant to our discussion. *The first is that He is the perfect Mediator*. While on the one hand Jesus is described as 'the Lord of all', with the New Testament writers quite deliberately using the personal name for God (Yahweh) to refer to Him, He is also spoken of in solidly human terms. He is 'Jesus' — a real historical man, 'of Nazareth' — a real historical place. These facts are put together theologically in the claim that Jesus was fully man and fully God. As such He is properly equipped to stand with ordinary people and hold their hands, and at the same time to stand alongside God the Father and bring the two sides together. It is because of this that the Gospel is described as 'Good News of peace by Jesus Christ.' He reconciles.

The New Testament speaks very negatively of people who follow their own manmade religions. They are described as now being under the wrath of God. I am told endlessly that the heathen are 'happy as they are', but the fact is that they do not know the living God. Their religions, which of course have some elements of truth mixed up in the muddle of error, are not able to bring them to the personal relationship with God for which they are made. People need to be made right with God, and the long list of mediators in many of the world's religions give eloquent testimony to this need. But when you examine these mediators you find that they fall short of what is needed to bring men and God together. Either the story is of one who is divine but not human — and therefore cannot

take hold of my hand to bring me to God; or
he is human but not divine — and therefore
can identify with me but not bring me to God.
Or, and very commonly, there are no
historical reasons for believing that the
mediator exists at all. And a story cannot save
us.

*The second important element of the Gospel
is that Jesus has power over the Devil.* He was
proclaimed as One who healed all oppressed
by the Devil, and went about doing good.

As you look out into the world you see
endless problems of devilish oppression. It
used to be common practice in the West to
ridicule the whole concept of the demonic.
The other day my boys came home from
primary school speaking of a group of
children who had tried to make contact with
the spirits during the lunch hour. This is an
increasingly common phenomenon. All over
Britain one hears of the revival of witchcraft.
The church of a friend of mine was daubed
and cursed by a coven of witches. A group in
another city are committed to the destruction
of Christian marriages; others claim to have
brought all sorts of harm upon certain
members of communities. The demonic seems
to be having something of a revival in the
West.

In many parts of the world it has never lost
control. Throughout Thailand the spirit shelf
is to be seen. Even outside modern airline
offices in the heart of technological society,

the spirit house is conspicuous. People still live with a need to appease the spirits.

A Filipino medical student travelled to her tribal home in the mountains in the north of the Philippines. Her parents, under the guidance of a demon spirit, made the girl identify herself with a pig, which was then slaughtered in her place. She was given a new name since she had 'died' when the pig died, and as a new person she was ritually married to her own father. I still tremble to think of the terrifying spiritual darkness that came over that girl and the trauma she went through when she returned to her studies at the modern medical faculty. The demonic is a real problem, far wider than remote primitive tribes.

There are recognized exorcists in every sort of religion. Devils can be cast out and people can be healed, without the deliverance actually doing the person any good.

A German woman went for healing to a spirit medium in the Philippines, and her complaint apparently improved. She said she was healed. But as a result she lost all interest in prayer and Bible study. Like Esau with his bowl of soup, she was satisfied with the meeting of a temporary physical need — and the price was the loss of the blessing of God. Only Jesus brings *good* deliverance.

Soon after a young man from Thailand was converted here in Scotland, he had a dream, during which he was being pursued by the demon god. He was offered something to protect him — a beautiful cross on which a golden Buddha was impaled. Three times he rejected this as a means of protection. In the dream he affirmed that it was the living Lord Jesus in his heart who was his protection — and Jesus alone.

A woman lay demon possessed in one of the best hospitals in Manila, a fine teaching hospital in which many students from the West were also enrolled. Several doctors sought to treat her with drugs and medical counselling. There was no change. Then a group of superstitious people, who had probably watched the film 'The Exorcist', put crucifixes and the like around the room. Nobody was helped. When the elders from a Christian church prayed and commanded the spirits to come out in the name of Jesus, she was delivered. Jesus brings good deliverance from the Devil. And when He heals it does good as well.

Like your girl friend, I once talked with a Filipino who said that she had prayed to St Martin for healing, and received it. Later she told me that whenever she prayed to St Martin it worked, but when she prayed to Jesus it never worked. The Devil does not mind giving the occasional blessing if by so doing he reinforces the barriers between that person and a saving relationship with Christ.

So we must not simply look at what works but at what does good in the long run. That is often hard to judge. So we are brought back again to the question, 'What is the truth?'

Another crucial area of the Gospel is that Jesus has power over sin. The fact that 'they put him to death by hanging him on a tree' is an essential part of the Gospel. It is through the crucifixion of Jesus that people can receive forgiveness of sins, for it is there that Jesus paid for sin once and for all.

The picture of Filipinos crawling on their knees towards statues of the saints as a way to be cleansed from sin is deeply impressed on my memory. I once joined a crowd of tens of thousands waiting in Manila for a statue of a black Christ carrying His cross. A well-educated man, a race-horse owner, began to explain to me what people believed about this statue. He said that it was widely held that those who managed to touch the statue or to have it dragged over their shoulders would receive a year's forgiveness. He described it in a detached way, as though he himself did not really believe it. But when the statue drew near he excused himself, saying that he must touch it if at all possible. One of my colleagues talked with men there who had committed themselves to walk through the streets every Good Friday lashing their backs open with whips. It was, they said, to pay for their sin.

Again and again one finds people subjecting themselves to all sorts of terrible indignities in the hope that they might find forgiveness and

peace with God. You can read up for yourself
about the desperate and tormenting penances
that some Hindus will undergo in the hope of
making merit and so having a better future
life.

I think that often we irreligious Westerners
do not appreciate how urgent forgiveness really
is. When Isaiah went for worship in the
Temple, there is no suggestion that he felt
particularly bad about things. But when he
saw the Lord as He really is, he shook with
terror. 'Woe is me! for I am lost; for I am a
man with unclean lips, and I dwell in the
midst of a people of unclean lips; for my eyes
have seen the King, the Lord of hosts!' (Isaiah
6.5) When he saw God he recognized that
even just his conversation left him in grave
danger. There is no evidence that by everyday
standards Isaiah was a particularly dirty-
mouthed person. His conversation would
probably have caused little trouble to the
average BBC censor — he would not have
needed to blot out any of Isaiah's words on an
interview! But God's holiness is of a very
much higher standard than so-called British
respectability. When God draws near, people
realize that they are not nice after all — and
that they are in danger.

So, the son of a senior Government official
in Nepal told me that when he tried to pray
there was as it were a veil hanging between
him and God, and he could not get through.
A delightful Korean post-graduate responded

in a Bible study, 'but I am too dirty to come
near to God.' A Filipino journalist who had
previously seemed so carefree in his
committed atheism, wept in horror as he tried
to pray to the God he had become convinced
was there. 'Why didn't you tell me it would
be so terrible to meet God?' he said.

In other words, when God draws near to
people they do not feel at ease. They're much
more likely to respond as did Peter when he'd
had a glimpse of the power of Jesus, 'Depart
from me, for I am a sinful man, O Lord'
(Luke 5.8).

Now if that is so, the most crucial thing that
people need is a Saviour from sin. People in
so many religions make penances and sin-
offerings as a tragic proclamation that they
need the real thing, the sin offering that is
enough. And that of course is Jesus, who died
in our place to pay the penalty of our sin. 'All
we like sheep have gone astray; we have
turned everyone to his own way; and the Lord
has laid on him the iniquity of us all' (Isaiah
53.6).

Islam of course seeks to compliment Jesus
by saying that He was too good and holy a
prophet to have suffered crucifixion. God
would not allow that. So Mohammed invented
a pious fiction whereby Jesus escaped
crucifixion and Judas was crucified instead.

Saul, the Jew, came at it from the other
way. He said that because Jesus had been
crucified He could not possibly have been

good and holy. Crucifixion was a sign of the
curse of God upon a man.

But both the Jewish and the Muslim errors
are corrected in the Word of God. Jesus
'redeemed us from the curse of the law,
having become a curse *for us* — for it is
written "Cursed be every one who hangs on a
tree" —' (Galatians 3.13). He was good and
holy, and He was bearing the curse of God.
But that was for us, in our place, instead of
us. That is why He is the answer to the sin
problem. That is why forgiveness is to be
found by people who trust Jesus. We need to
recognize that while other religions attempt to
pay for sin, only Jesus could make a sufficient
sacrifice actually to do it.

More than that, Jesus is the Saviour who
works BOTH sides of death. And there is no
evidence that any other religion can deal with
that problem. We'll talk about that some
other time.

I was so pleased to hear you are still going
steady with your Rachel — and that you are
both getting involved in cross-cultural witness.
Rose and I really got to know each other well
when we ran a holiday for overseas students
in 1968. (Was it really so long ago?!) We
hired two caravans — one for the women and
the other for the men — fourteen of us from
eleven different countries! And hardly any of
them Christians. We were constantly
nicknamed 'Mummy and Daddy' and
eventually . . . need I say more?! The

wonderful extra blessings of cross-cultural
witness! Keep at it, Paul.

Rose joins me in sending our love to you
both,

Your brother,
DICK.

9

BUT MISSIONARIES AREN'T WELCOME

Dear Dick,

Rachel and I have been praying much recently about what we should be doing with our lives. As you know, we went along to one of your missionary conferences and were greatly challenged by the reports of the different missionaries. Those Bible Readings from Isaiah certainly hit very hard too.

Since we have been home a number of questions have come into our minds, especially when we have thought about the whole business of church-planting ministry in Asia. We have been very struck with the way that so many different people have spoken about the problems of getting into countries for missionary work these days. While we were at the conference news reached us that the Thai Supreme Command has now banned missionary work among the different refugee groups in Thailand. We already knew that it was pretty difficult to get missionaries in to reach the Thai. There seem to be precious few ways in which missionaries can get into Indonesia. Malaysia doesn't appear to want them, and you seem to have to wait an awful

long time to get proper visas for people in the
Philippines. Vietnam, Laos, Cambodia,
Burma are all closed as far as missionary work
is concerned. There may be a crack in the door
into China, but it is hardly an opening for the
preaching of the Gospel in the normal sense of
the word.

All this seems to be saying that people do
not want missionaries. And I can't really say
that I blame them. After all, they have been
getting on fine since time immemorial. Now in
come these strange 'whites' with their foreign
religion, causing all sorts of problems and
bother.

Yes, we do believe that they need to hear the
Gospel. But if they don't want it, then what
can we do?

The other problem in our minds is this. Is it
really appropriate for us as foreigners to go
and tell these people that they have got it all
wrong, that they are on the road to Hell, and
that they need to accept our religion if they are
going to have any hope at all? It all sounds
horribly arrogant. Surely it would come much
better from a national.

We are prepared to go as missionaries. But
we don't want to force ourselves on people
who don't want us. It doesn't seem right
somehow to go where you are not welcome,
and it certainly is very difficult to be asked to
tell people whose language we hardly know
and whose culture we don't understand that
they have got it all wrong.

Having said that, we do want to serve the Lord. And we are prepared to go anywhere He leads us. We should greatly appreciate your prayers for guidance as we think about our future life together.

With warm greetings in Christ,
PAUL.

Dear Paul and Rachel,

I really feel that I must include Rachel in this now, since you are thinking it through together!

What a joy it was to learn of your willingness to go anywhere for the sake of the Lord Jesus. Too many of us these days are laying down the limits of our discipleship. We want the Lord to show us His will, and then promise to consider it! Only those who are committed to unconditional discipleship really discover the joy of the Lord, I believe.

But I'm alarmed that you think missionary work is only valid when people give the missionaries an enthusiastic welcome. If Jesus had waited for the world to welcome Him He would still be waiting to be born in Bethlehem. He experienced widespread rejection. At other times people gave Him an initial welcome, only to quit later when they realized the demands of His discipleship. I don't think anyone has ever been as

unwelcome as Jesus was when He came for
our salvation. The angels may have turned out
in force to welcome Him, but precious few
people did. And the loneliness at the climax
of His ministry was unbelievable.

Jesus didn't offer us a different experience.
'If the world hates you,' He said, 'know that
it has hated me before it hated you' (John
15.18). On the last night before the crucifixion
He begged His Father to keep His disciples
from the Evil One, saying, 'I have given them
Thy Word; and the world has hated them
because they are not of the world, even as I
am not of the world' (John 17.14). In the
Sermon on the Mount He even suggested that
persecution could lead to a form of assurance.
'Blessed are you when men revile you and
persecute you . . . on my account. Rejoice
and be glad, . . . *for so men persecuted the
prophets who were before you*' (Matthew 5.10-
12). All those who brought a prophetic word
to people could have been stamped with the
same slogan: 'Not Welcome'.

The question is not, 'Do they want
missionaries?' but 'Do they need the Gospel?'
And I reckon you know that they do. Most of
us, and most other people in the world, like
to be left just the way we are. The New
Testament said this is because 'men loved
darkness rather than light, because their deeds
were evil' (John 3.19). If that is right, we
should be foolish to expect a welcome.

When God accepted Isaiah as a volunteer

worker, he gave him a horrific job-
description. He told him that there would be
almost no response to his ministry. Most
people would hear it but never really get the
message. They would watch him ministering
but never really understand the point of it all.
When Isaiah realized quite how tough his
assignment was, he immediately asked how
long he would be required to do it. Perhaps
he wanted to know if he could do it 'for a few
months, before settling down' as some
students put it to me. God's answer was
alarming. He wanted the job done until there
was nobody left in the houses to be reached
with the message (See Isaiah 6).

As long as there are people who need to
hear, God wants messengers to take the
message to them. And the commitment is not
to be short-term. It is to be until there is no
one left to reach. They may not want to hear,
but they need to hear. And God wants them
to hear.

Ezekiel was similarly told that he had to
discharge the message 'whether they hear or
refuse to hear' (Ezekiel 3.11). We are not
answerable for doors slammed in the face of
the Gospel, but we are answerable if we never
bother to try the door.

It is true that in the New Testament Jesus
encouraged the disciples to shake the dust off
their feet when villages proved unresponsive
to them and their message (Luke 10.10-12).
But it is doubtful whether this should be a

universal practice today. The disciples then
were engaged on a brief mission, preparing
the way for a visit by Jesus Himself. In later
days the work of the Gospel was likened to
farming — breaking up the ground, planting,
watering, and reaping. That implies a much
longer-term commitment. Thus, the first
twenty years of evangelistic work among the
Thai Muslims in the South of Thailand
resulted in only one person being converted.
But much ground was prepared and much
sowing done. Only now is there the beginning
of a reaping work.

I have on my desk a leaflet about the life
and work of Koos Fietje, who was murdered
last year while ministering as an evangelist
among the people of Central Thailand. In the
course of an address to new missionaries just
a week before Koos was shot and killed, he
said, 'Today I will live to glorify God . . . I
will live each day as though it were my last. I
am ready to go home at any time.' We need
many more men who are prepared to risk
their physical lives for the sake of the eternal
needs of people who just do not want to know
— but need to.

I do appreciate your concern about the
problems of being a foreigner and of the
offence that foreigners can so easily cause by
criticizing things. It is so easy to say the
wrong thing, or even to say the right thing in
the wrong way or in a way which is
misunderstood.

Only the other day I had a very difficult interview with a Thai mother who was upset and angry at her daughter's Christian discipleship. At one point in the discussion, to my horror, she evidently concluded that I was making offensive remarks about the King of Thailand. In fact nothing could have been further from my intention. I have great admiration for the King of Thailand. But I was misunderstood and misinterpreted in a way that would never have been the case if I had been Thai and spoken fluent Thai.

Yes, there are real problems of communication and cultural adaptation when you are a foreign missionary. But there are sometimes advantages as well. A Japanese friend who was helped on in his Christian life in an English university once wrote to me from Tokyo. The burden of his letter was about the problem of evangelizing as a Japanese in Japan. He claimed that if the person was his superior, then it was his duty to agree with him or at least to appear to do so. On the other hand if the person was his inferior, then it would be that person's duty at least to appear to agree with his superior. This, said my friend, made evangelism extremely difficult.

As a matter of fact, I know many Japanese who have overcome this problem. But I think it is true to say that it is not a problem the foreign missionary experiences in quite the same way. In a sense he stands outside this cultural requirement.

Of course, on the debit side the Japanese language is so terribly difficult that the foreigner may well be unable to take up the cultural advantages for evangelism because he cannot express himself fluently enough!

Be that as it may, it is not biblical to argue that evangelism is *always* best done by a person of the same race as those who need to be reached. Many here in Scotland were greatly helped by the ministry of the Argentinian evangelist Luis Palau. While some have argued that the work in Scotland should be done by a Scot, or within the confines of the local Scottish denominations, others do testify to the fact that the foreigner communicated where they had never apparently heard the message before.

Certainly the obligation to make disciples of all nations does not belong to any one nationality. It belongs to the church all over the world. Every church has that responsibility. God has an urgent place for cross-cultural communication in the building of His Church. Don't think of this as a necessary evil for the present. It is an essential element in the life of every mature and growing church.

So missionaries are needed from your country to go to the nations. But you are greatly mistaken and terribly out of date if you think of all missionaries as Westerners. Most of the original missionaries were from

the Middle East. During the last century and
the first half of this century most missionaries
did come from Western Europe and North
America. But in these days it is exciting to see
many Asian, African and some Latin
American churches waking up to their
obligation to fulfil the Great Commission. As
a result we are seeing much more truly
international missionary work, and this is of
tremendous advantage for the work of the
Gospel in those countries where Western
missionaries are labelled with all the stigma of
Western imperialism and where the Gospel is
wrongly thought of as a Western religion.
International teams of missionaries help show
this is not so.

I appreciate your point that nobody likes to
be told that they are wrong by a foreigner.
The Western press makes much of the
notorious sexual vice of a city like Bangkok.
But this criticism does not sound good to the
Thai when he observes Western businessmen
and service men taking advantage of the
facilities of the 'red light' districts. The
Western missionary might with reason be told
not to come and tell the Thai about their sin,
but rather, 'Go home and tell your own
people about the sin that they commit!'

This was precisely the comment that was
hurled at the prophet Amos when he brought
God's Word to Israel. 'Go home to Judah,
and tell them the word of God', said
Amaziah, the heretical religious leader. But

Amos was not to go home to Judah. God had
called him out of his market gardening
business to take the Word to Israel. Certainly
Judah needed to hear what God had to say
about its sin and its need. But that was not
Amos's job. Amos's job was to deliver a word
to the country next door. And woe betide that
country if it did not listen.

In a sense Amos's safeguard was his call to
such missionary service. He was not a self-
appointed missionary. He was not in it for the
money. He did not do it because there was
nothing better to do. He had been called out
of a perfectly good job. He had been called
away from a country that nonetheless needed
to hear the Word of God. He was called by
God to Israel — and so Israel needed to listen
to God's Word through him.

How important it was that Amos stuck to
what God was saying! When we were working
among nationalistic Filipino students they
would often ask us, 'Is that British or
biblical?' If it was British then they simply
were not interested. And that was right. Our
job was not to go as cultural imperialists but
as missionaries of the Word of God. The
message you have to deliver is what God's
Word says to the country you are called to go
to. They do not need the British way of life.
But they do need God's answers.

This is really the key to the whole question.
If we believe that people are in very urgent
need of the Gospel, we shall go to them

whether they welcome us or not. If we really believe that God's Word has the answers, and the only answers, to save people from Hell, then we shall want to share with them whatever the national and cultural differences may be. The real question is this: do we believe that the alternative to the Gospel is Hell?

Because Paul believed in the wrath of God, he reckoned that he was absolutely obliged to share the Gospel with people. 'I am under obligation both to Greeks and to barbarians, both to the wise and to the foolish: so I am eager to preach the gospel to you also who are in Rome' (Romans 1.14-15). If people are really that lost, then we too are under a tremendous obligation. And our burden cannot be for Britain only or for just one type of people. The burden for the lost stretches to all those who have not heard the Gospel.

So strong was this sense of obligation that Paul reckoned that he was doing no one a favour by preaching the Gospel to them. He said, 'Necessity is laid upon me. Woe to me if I do not preach the gospel!' (1 Cor. 9.16) 'I am not doing you Corinthians a favour. I'd be in big trouble if I didn't tell you the Gospel.'

Having written that, I am deeply conscious of the fact that often I do not talk to people about Jesus. I know far too little of the urgent sense of evangelistic compulsion which kept the apostle Paul working. I am sure that in part this is because the truths about which I

am writing have still not really gripped my
own heart and imagination. I would like you
to pray that the Lord will give to us as a
family a real burden for lost people. The boys
have school friends with Muslim names. Wee
Rachel goes to play school with a girl named
after an African fertility goddess. I long that
the children too should be able to commend
Jesus persuasively as the only Saviour.

And I long too for urgent and daring
outreach from our congregations. I was
talking to a minister this morning. He told me
that there were no foreigners in his
congregation apart from one Hungarian. As I
drove back from church last night I was struck
by the numbers of Pakistanis on the streets,
but for all my travelling around Scotland I
have yet to preach in a church with people of
Pakistani origin worshipping Jesus in the
congregation.

If we really believe in the doctrine of Hell,
then surely we have to plan for action to
reach such lost peoples.

I wonder where you are planning to live
when you get married? Your home could be
the centre of a new and significant outreach
into an unevangelized community. In New
Testament days Aquila and Priscilla had that
sort of vision — they started congregations in
their homes in Italy, Greece and Turkey. You
might pioneer a work among Pakistanis from
your first home here in Glasgow. How about
it? It would be super to have you around and

to have the chance of more regular face to face fellowship with you.

But what matters is what God has planned for your life together. Do not spend time fretting over the 'problem' of guidance. If you are walking with the Lord, then He is committed (in writing!) to guide you, *WHEN YOU NEED TO KNOW* (see Proverbs 3.5-6). He could hardly have said that He made us Christians 'for a life of good deeds, which he has already prepared for us to do' (Ephesians 2.10 GNB) if He was then going to make it more or less impossible for us to discover what those plans are. Do what you know He wants now — and leave Him to show the next step at the right time.

The Lord gave me six months notice to go to the Philippines. Then He gave us as a family three weeks clear notice to come to Scotland. And it was enough . . . just!

The problem is not guidance — but obedience. When we thought God might want us to move to Scotland, Andrew (then 5) prayed, 'Lord, if you want us to go to Scotland, please make it that we go — and don't argue about it.' So we did as we were told — and discovered once again that the will of God for us is indeed 'good, and acceptable, and perfect'. Funny that we should think otherwise really!

With much love in the Lord Jesus.

Yours sincerely,

DICK.

10

IT'S AN UNFAIR WORLD

Dear Dick,
My mother phoned earlier today and
dropped something of a bombshell. She told
me that my Aunt Angela has terminal cancer.
Apparently they rushed her into hospital last
week for what she thought was going to be a
preliminary investigation, but they just did an
open-and-shut operation because the cancer
was so extensive that nothing can be done.

This has been particularly distressing because
Aunt Angela has been rather special to me
over the years. She looked after me when I was
a child and my mother was ill. In a funny sort
of way she has been more of a mother to me
than my own mum. It is almost as though I
hurt with her hurt at the moment, I feel so
bound up with her in the trauma of all this.

Honestly, Dick, it seems so unfair. She has
always been such a delightful person. She is
kind. She has always cared for people going
through a rough time, and yet never gives the
impression of being a 'do-good-er'. No, I
know what you're going to ask, she is not a
Christian. In fact she has some very odd
religious views. But she has never said
anything negative about my Christian faith.

She is tolerant and sincere, and I think she really lives up to the light that she has.

Why, then, should God let this happen to her?

This question has really been bugging me. And the more I have thought about it, the more I find myself concluding that the majority of people who suffer in the world are innocent and don't deserve it.

For example, most of the multitudes that the Red Guard got rid of during the Cultural Revolution in China were not terrible criminals, they were nice ordinary Chinese people — the sort of people that China would be glad to have around these days. The terrible suffering that tens of thousands experienced in Cambodia under Pol Pot was surely not because they had been specially wicked. They were ordinary, innocent Khmer. What did the six million Jews who died in the last war do wrong? Most of them died for no other reason than that Hitler did not like them. Even among my own neighbours here, I can think of tons of nice people who go through horrible experiences that they really do not deserve.

I find it too hard to believe that those who have had such a raw deal in this life will go to Hell when they die, just because they are not Christians. God is a just God. Surely this innocent suffering counts for something in His eyes. Surely those who have had to go through so much here on earth can look forward to something better in the life to come.

Yes, I know it is my job to share the Gospel with suffering people. I know it would be much better and that their suffering would be more manageable if they had a living relationship with Jesus. But as far as Aunt Angela is concerned, I do not really think she is in a fit state to listen to the Gospel any more. And time is running out anyway.

There must be a way for her to be all right. Please help me to understand. And please be gentle. This has ceased to be an academic discussion. It matters to me in a way that it never has before. I would to God that I were the one who had the cancer instead of her — I could at least look forward to Heaven with some assurance.

Do pass on my love in the Lord to Rose. A mutual friend told me that she is still having a good bit of trouble with the colitis problem. It is strange that the pain has gone on nagging for so many years despite our prayers. I am sure that she doesn't deserve extra suffering. It must be bad enough coping with you and the kids and everything else that gets landed on her plate, without having that as well. (Sorry that sounds rather ruder than it was meant to be — but you know what I mean.)

God bless — and please try to write soon.
PAUL.

Dear Paul,

I'm so sorry to learn of the horrible illness of your Aunt. I am grieved too to know something of the trauma that you are going through at this time.

Over these weeks we have written so much about the need of unconverted people. In some ways we have been quite detached in our discussion. But now you are beginning to *feel* the horror of Hell, instead of just thinking about it. Somehow it is easier for us to talk in terms of millions dying without Christ, than it is to talk of the urgent spiritual need of Aunt Angela.

Perhaps in some respects the Lord puts a brake on our emotions. If we felt as moved as you do for Aunt Angela over all the unevangelized millions in the world, I think we would just crack up. On the other hand, it is a terrible thing that most of the time we care so little about the needs of unconverted people. The Lord once had to challenge Jonah sternly. He had become all steamed up and depressed about the death of a plant, but he had not been moved at all by the lostness of the thousands who lived in Nineveh. That was what moved God. And it didn't just stir His heart, it stirred Him into action.

Maybe, through your tears for Aunt Angela, you will begin a little more to feel as God feels, like Jesus cried over Jerusalem.

I do not think you want me to give you long theological answers at the moment. But I do think that you need to face the facts as they are. In the long run, there is no real help gained by running off into Cloud Cuckoo-Land.

The first fact is that Aunt Angela is going to die. If the cancer follows its normal course she will die quite soon. If she were to be granted a remission, and of course everybody is hoping for that, she will still die. That is one of the few things in life from which none of us is exempt. We have all got to face it sooner or later.

The second fact is that she does not belong to Jesus. That is something you are sure about. You know the consequences of that as well as I do.

I put those two things down in cold print because nobody's going to be helped by pretence. If she is going to die — you have got to face that. If she is not a Christian, you have got to face that too, otherwise you will not do the right things for her or anyone else. We must not look for comfort and security in lies and wishful thinking.

Of course it is true that we do not all get equal portions of suffering. Some of us have a rough time of it; others have it pretty easy. We live together in a fallen world among sinners like ourselves — and that means problems. I must admit that I do not altogether understand why the problems are distributed so unevenly. But they are.

I've been greatly helped recently by reading

Joni Eareckson's two books 'Joni' and 'A Step Further'.[1] Her testimony as a woman more or less paralysed from the neck downwards is powerful reading. And her biblical insights into the problem of suffering are among the most helpful that I have read. It is easy to read too — which is a help, when you are feeling pretty strung up.

One of the things that comes over so clearly in Joni's books is this: if only you are walking with God, you will find that He gives the measure of help that you need in order to cope with the amount of suffering you are going through. Though it sometimes does not seem quite like that, on looking back you can see that He does not allow you to have problems beyond your strength. (2 Cor. 1.3-5; 1 Cor. 10.13) With the assurance that 'in *everything* God works for good with those who love him' (Romans 8.28), Joni is able to write of the *blessing* of suffering.

I must confess that we have not always seen clearly the blessings that God has brought through suffering. When Rose was first so critically ill in the Philippines, her ministry was redirected from campus evangelism (for which she did not have the physical strength any more) to the training of Filipino Christian workers from the base of our home. There is no doubt that this was, in the long-term, a much more strategic ministry. But she would

[1] Published by Zondervan (USA) and P & I (Glasgow).

never have been shut up to it if she hadn't been knocked about physically. That doesn't mean that we have got nice easy answers for the considerable discomfort that she still experiences from time to time.

I might be tempted to ask why the amoebae in the Manila water supply ate so enthusiastically into the lining of Rosemary's colon while they left mine alone. I could well argue that since I am more sinful, I should have experienced greater suffering. But it is not as simple as that. If that were so, Jesus would have sailed through life on earth without a single problem or the slightest hurt.

This is a sad and broken world. Sin, suffering, frustration, disease, death and alienation can all be traced to the mess that Adam started. And we have all had a part in mucking up God's world and hurting one another.

Having messed it up, we've still got to live in it. And we have still got to live with one another. We are not self-contained units, we are inter-dependent — for good or for ill. God designed it for good — for family life, fellowship, love, a secure society. But when people choose what is wrong, they are not the only ones who get hurt. The blessing of being bound up together backfires, and lots who have not chosen that sin get hurt by it (as did the Jews because of Hitler's wicked thinking). Moreover, when people spoil the environment, everybody else has got to live in it — with the consequences.

It is a messed-up world that produces cancer. It is a rebel society that rejects God's answers when suffering. Your Aunt Angela belongs to this spoilt world, and the responsibility for her problem cannot simply be laid at her feet. It is not God's fault either. The blame belongs here on earth — but it would be pretty futile to try and name names.

Both for your aunt and for the others you mention, I have to agree that the suffering was not their fault. But that doesn't mean that we can talk about them as 'innocent' sufferers. There has only ever been one innocent sufferer in the world, and that was the Lord Jesus. Apart from Him, nobody is innocent. Indeed, though it sounds terrible to say it, God would not be unfair if he damned us all now. Even the worst suffering that we see here on earth is nothing compared with what we sinners deserve.

For all that, God still cares. He sent Jesus, His only Son, to deliver us from the worst suffering. There is no need to be at odds with God and cut off from Him for ever. When you know God, suffering takes on a completely different perspective. The Christian does not escape suffering. But he has amazing help in and through it, and when he dies the deliverance is gloriously complete.

When some time ago an elder at our church died of cancer and this was explained to young David, his response was: 'Wow! How

wonderful for him! Now he can see Jesus.
And the Lord Jesus is going to give him a
new body which won't hurt any more!' That is
the hope that God offers now for those who
will take His way of salvation.

Look, Paul, we really cannot assume that
there is a back door for those who have it
rough here on earth.

One of the visions in Scripture that I find
particularly unnerving is that of the day of the
wrath of God and of the Lamb (Rev. 6.12-
17). The picture is of people wishing that they
could be buried alive in an earthquake rather
than have to face God and the Lord Jesus
Christ. By then, there is no more opportunity
to turn to God. While it concentrates on the
fate of great men, rich men, generals and
others, it also reveals that 'everyone, slave
and free' will experience the same terror. You
might want to argue that the slaves who were
cruelly exploited and had no rights, privileges
or good things to enjoy, should be able to
look forward to a better after-life. But that is
not what Scripture says. If they are not
reached for Christ before they die or He
comes, there is no hope for them either.

When, in the Bible, people who loved the
Lord saw that judgment was coming on those
they loved, they gave themselves to urgent
prayer. Abraham felt for Sodom and
Gomorrah — his own nephew, Lot, was
there. So he undertook the most moving time
of intercession on behalf of the people of that

city. He was even prepared to provoke the anger of God against himself if only some from those lost communities might be spared (Gen. 18.20-33).

When Moses realized that the wrath of God was to fall upon his idolatrous fellow-countrymen, and perhaps even upon his own brother Aaron, he prayed fervently. He did not dispute the fact that they deserved Hell. But he longed to persuade God to save them. 'If not, blot me, I pray thee, out of Thy book which Thou hast written' (Exodus 32.32).

The apostle Paul wrote in the same vein about his burden for his kinsmen. 'I am speaking the truth in Christ, I am not lying; my conscience bears me witness in the Holy Spirit, that I have great sorrow and unceasing anguish in my heart. For I could wish that I myself were accursed and cut off from Christ for the sake of my brethren, my kinsmen by race' (Romans 9.1-3). 'My heart's desire and prayer to God for them is that they may be saved,' he said (Romans 10.1). He did not think they would be saved because of their zeal. It was a misguided zeal. He did not believe they could plead ignorance. They did not want the truth. He knew that they could not argue on the basis of their morality, because he was clear that good works do not save. He did not pretend there is no Hell. He wished that he could go there in place of his brethren if only that would save them. But it could not. The way ahead was to pray.

J.O. Fraser, who worked among the Lisu in China, regarded the work of prayer as the most essential element in moving people to respond. He once wrote, 'I find myself able to do little or nothing apart from God's going before me and working among men. Without this I feel like a man who has his boat grounded in shallow water. Pull or push as he may, he will not be able to make his boat move more than a few inches. But let the tide come in and lift his boat off the bottom — then he will be able to move it as far as he pleases, quite easily and without friction. It is indeed necessary for me to go around among our Lisu, preaching, teaching, exhorting, rebuking, but the amount of progress made thereby depends almost entirely on the state of the Spiritual Tide in the village — a condition which you can control upon your knees as well as I can'[1].

Prayer does not automatically save people. Abraham saw very little answer to his earnest intercession. But I believe that, if anyone is converted, someone has normally prayed down the blessing of God. This is because God likes to work *with us* as His colleagues. And that is certainly nothing for us to complain about. It is a wonderful privilege.

It is not yet time for you to say that it is too late for Aunt Angela. At the very least we must pray that the Lord will open her heart to

[1] *The Prayer of Faith* (OMF) page 9.

the Gospel, even though she is far gone.

Then, I do think it would be appropriate to look for an opportunity to talk to her some more about the Lord Jesus. It may be that her time of opportunity has already passed. I do not know. But if she is dying, even if the doctors have not got the courage to tell her, she probably has a pretty good idea what is going on. Usually death is the one thing that nobody will talk about. But people normally have things that they want to put right if they know that they haven't got long to live. And quite often it *is* an opportunity to talk gently and humbly of the Saviour who conquered death.

Even when a person is apparently unconscious, it is surprising what they can hear. I have friends who have shared the Gospel with unconscious people, who have then come round and made a profession of faith.

A missionary colleague of ours once forgot this when standing next to Rose's bed when she was not far from death's door. Thinking she could not hear because she appeared to be unconscious, he turned to his wife and said, 'I don't reckon she'll last more than another couple of days, do you?' Rose heard him — and afterwards thought it was very funny!

I don't mean by all this that you should barge in and force the Gospel down her throat. But I mean that you have no right to

assume it is too late. If it was not too late for
the thief on the cross to put his trust in the
Saviour, then we can be sure that God
welcomes those who repent even in the last
minute of their lives (Luke 23.42-43). People
who think that salvation is a matter of being
good and trying hard find this sort of thing
rather repugnant. But in fact we contribute
nothing to our salvation except (as William
Temple put it) the sin from which we need to
be saved. And people converted at the last
minute are a wonderful advertisement in the
heavenlies among the angels and others of the
amazing grace of God in Christ.

I want you to know, Paul, that as well as
praying for Aunt Angela, we shall be praying
for you. I have no way of knowing what is
going on in your Aunt. I can only long and
pray and hope — not fully understanding
God's purposes in it all. But I do know that
other members of the family will be watching
you to see how you will cope with this
trauma.

I'm sure that God will help you through
this, and I know that one of the purposes of
His helping you is so that you will be able to
help others in similar difficulties. (2 Cor.
1.3ff). Jesus, who cried over the lostness of
His kinsmen in Jerusalem, understands the
trauma that you are going through. So it is
good to draw near to Him now.

I think this is really too long a letter to
have written to you at such a difficult time.

But I know you are keeping this correspondence, and you may want to get it out later and think these things through again then.

'Who among you fears the LORD and obeys the voice of His servant, who walks in darkness and has no light, yet trusts in the name of the LORD and relies upon his God?' (Isaiah 50.10) Hold tight *in the dark*.

Rose joins me in sending our love to you. God bless.

DICK.

11

SHE DIED — AND I LOVED HER ·

Dear Dick,

I'm sorry that I haven't written to you for so long. As you may have seen in the newspaper, Aunt Angela died just a day or two after I received your last letter. Since then I've felt a strange mixture of shattered, numb, guilty and depressed. By and large I've tried to battle through with my feelings on my own. I certainly haven't felt up to writing them down for you. But now I think I had better make contact again because I don't seem to be making too much headway.

As far as I know, she never put her trust in Jesus as her Saviour. I almost wish that we had never begun this correspondence because I have seen much too clearly in the Scriptures the terrible consequences of not being a Christian. I wanted to believe that there was some sort of back door. But I know that is wishful thinking, and that knowledge has left an awful black shadow of horror hanging over me. You see, Dick, I believe that she is lost forever. That is a terrible thing to write of someone who has been very special to me, someone who has helped me more than anybody else I know.

But that is only half of the problem. The

other part of it is this. I have been close to her for years, and I have been a Christian for some time now. If anyone had opportunity to win her for Christ, it was I. If anyone had opportunity to explain the Gospel to her, I did. But I failed. My attempts at witnessing were so feeble. She really did not have a chance. I can think of quite a number of occasions when I could have talked more directly about her need of Jesus Christ. But I was a coward. I did not want to be embarrassed. I let Jesus down. And I sent her to Hell.

This has really tormented me over the last few weeks.

When I received your letter I was so excited about the possibility of her yet being converted. How I prayed! And I did actually have an opportunity to read the Bible to her and share something of my testimony. But she was not interested. I think she had too many other things on her mind by then. I do not think I shall ever be able to think about Aunt Angela without feeling terrible about the way that I let her down.

I had a short chat with the man who conducted the service at the crematorium. He hadn't a clue who she was; he just happened to be the minister on duty. So he just read through the service. I don't blame him. After all, they do them every twenty minutes, so the thing is bound to get a bit mechanical. I had a hunch he would not be of much help. But because he was there and I needed someone to

*talk to, I spoke to him anyway. I told him that
my Aunt was not prepared to meet God as her
judge and that I felt responsible for this.*

*He obviously didn't trust the Bible. He said
that nobody believes in judgment these days.
Jesus had believed in a judgment day and the
apostles agreed with Him during the early days
of the church. But, he reckoned, it was
something they all grew out of. I think he
believes that everyone is saved whether they
know about it or not.*

*So I didn't find talking to him very helpful.
But there was one thing he said that has stuck
in my mind. He reckoned that you and I
believe in a terrible God who doesn't really
love people but is only interested in His own
reputation.*

*Somehow this picture won't go away: God
as a sort of ogre just waiting to hurl people
into Hell. In my heart of hearts I know that He
is a God of love and of compassion. But I
cannot feel that any more. It is the feeling of
Him being an ogre that haunts me. And that
doesn't exactly help when it comes to prayer or
to worship. In fact that is really quite a battle
these days.*

*I am sorry to send you such a problem-
orientated letter. I seem to bounce between a
depressing feeling of guilt and a strong
temptation to hurl the blame at God.*

*It has been so good to have Rachel around
in all this chaos. She has listened so patiently
to my endless talk, and when I haven't felt up*

to it she has been super in helping me to pray.
It has just been nice to have someone around
who loves me, and who takes me as I am.

But she hasn't known how to answer some
of these questions. Perhaps you can give a bit
of help there. A couple of weeks ago I couldn't
have stomached a long letter; that's why I
didn't write. But now I do need some answers,
and hope that you will be able to write soon.
   With much love in Christ
   PAUL.

Dear Paul,
   I'm afraid I missed the news of your aunt's
sad death, though I did have a hunch that
something must have happened because of
your unusually long silence. We prayed in
response to that hunch, and are amazed to see
from your letter how accurately we were
guided in our praying.
   To begin with, I knew you would have to
battle with a sense of guilt because she did
not become a Christian. But I am not going to
join in the chorus of others who will tell you
that you mustn't blame yourself. From what
you have told me, you did in part fail to
present the Gospel to Aunt Angela.
Opportunities were missed because of lack of
vision or fear that you would look a bit of a
fool.
   If that is right then there is a *real* element

to your guilt. And that needs to be repented
of. Some people would say that is a very hard
thing to write to you at such a time as this.
But I know that you are not excusing
yourself, and I know that you need to call sin
by its name, as God does. That does not
mean you must live with this burden for the
rest of your life. God means you to settle it
with Him and be assured of His forgiveness.
When we agree with what God says about our
sin and turn from it, He promises to forgive
us and to make us clean from it all (1 John
1.9).

It is true that God considers the sin of
failing to tell someone the Gospel as serious
as murder. But if God could restore to David
the *joy* of His salvation after he had slept with
Bathsheba and murdered her husband Uriah,
then He can restore your joy as well.
However serious the sin, He can say, 'I will
remember their sin no more' (Jeremiah
31.34). That verse meant a tremendous
amount to me at a time when I wondered
whether God could ever use me again or even
really forgive me. We shall pray that God will
give you that sort of assurance too. If it is
settled, He has deliberately *forgotten* it!

One of the things you need to face is that if
Aunt Angela is lost for ever, it is because of
her sin and not because of yours. Ezekiel,
who was taught the solemn responsibility of
sharing the Word of God, also had to learn
that no one could blame someone else if he

were under the wrath of God. 'The soul that
sins shall die. The son shall not suffer for the
iniquity of the father, nor the father suffer for
the iniquity of the son . . .' (Ezekiel 18.20). If
she stands condemned before God, then the
Bible says that is her fault and not yours.
That again sounds terribly hard. But, just as
you must not excuse yourself for those things
for which God calls you to account, so you
must not blame yourself for those things for
which God does not condemn you.

The New Testament tells us that if our
hearts condemn us, God is greater than our
hearts (1 John 3.19-21). That is to say, we are
to repeat what God says in His Word rather
than what our own mixed-up ideas tell us. So
often when we are depressed we keep on
repeating things that are in fact untrue. We
need to keep putting the beautiful and lovely
and true things in our minds that God has
said. Then we will begin to have the peace of
God in our hearts (Philippians 4.8-9).

I think that one of the reasons it is very
hard to accept forgiveness when we have
badly let down somebody who has died, is
that we can hardly make amends for it. We
cannot apologize to the person who has died.
And we don't get a second chance to
evangelize him either.

Even so, there are things that you can do to
show the genuineness of your repentance. Are
there other people who are your
responsibility, to whom you have not

witnessed for a long time? Perhaps it would be good to make a list of their names and to begin to pray that God will give you the courage to take the opportunities that He gives you with them.

When I was a student, news came through of a Christian at a nearby university whose friend had asked him to stop work and help him with his problems. But he had a term paper to finish and said that he was too busy just then. The friend seeking help went away in despair and committed suicide.

When I heard that story I made a commitment before God to be available always for people who were seeking God or needing His help through their problems. The Lord used that brother's failure to bring me to a deeper commitment to evangelize. And I rather expect that he too was brought to a similar place of commitment.

I often think of the horror story of Jonah. He was a spiritual man, in touch with the Lord, and knowing His guidance. And God wanted him to carry a burden for lost Iraqis. Jonah was gifted as an evangelist — many sailors were converted when he spoke with them. But he would rather die than talk to Iraqis about the living God. God pursued him and he ran away to a Spanish holiday resort. And he really did get into a dreadful mess. Having been brought up on cod-liver oil, I can think of few more terrible fates than being in the belly of a big fish! Even his deliverance was messy. When Jonah prayed in repentance, God made the fish vomit him up on to the dry land. However, the point you need to get is this: Jonah was given another chance to evangelize Iraqis. I am sure that some had died in Nineveh while Jonah was on his joy-ride to Tarshish. But God gave Jonah a second chance to reach people there. And as a result many were converted and delivered from the judgment of God.

You cannot have a second chance with Aunt Angela. But I believe that God longs to give you many other opportunities to share the Gospel with people who urgently need to know the Saviour. Your experience has been painful. But you are not a write-off. You now have a profound sense of horror at what it means to die without Christ. God will use that to give you a sense of urgency which too few Christians have these days.

Now don't go overboard in a frantic evangelistic hit-and-run in all directions, will you? God has not made you the answer for the whole world! But He does expect you to be alert to opportunities to talk gladly and naturally about Jesus with friends and acquaintances, and with any others to whom the Lord clearly calls you!

The need of lost people was graphically brought home to me recently on the television news, when they showed film of a terrible hotel fire in Japan. You may have seen the movie, 'Towering Inferno'. That was just a

story, but this was the real thing. The film
cameras zoomed in on one desperate man
precariously balanced on a window-sill from
which he was rescued. Afterwards, he was
reported to have said, 'One false move and
I'd have dropped into Hell.'

Now I do not know how much Christian
doctrine that man had studied. But he lives in
a country where probably less than six people
in every thousand are Christians. So the
chances are that his remark about the danger
of Hell was right.

Wesley once wrote a fine hymn which
begins 'Give me the faith which can remove
and sink the mountain to a plain'. The second
verse of that hymn is normally conveniently
edited out of modern hymnbooks. It reads:

'I want an even strong desire,
I want a calmly fervent zeal,
To save poor souls out of the fire,
To snatch them from the verge of hell,
And turn them to a pardoning God,
And quench the brands in Jesu's blood.'

At least that Japanese fellow might have
appreciated Wesley's imagery!

But I'm not prepared to buy for a moment
the idea that God is a dreadful ogre delighting
in the damnation of unbelievers. When God
told Ezekiel that He would terribly judge
anyone who did not turn to Him in
repentance and faith, He leaned over
backwards in urgent pleading with them. 'Cast
away from you all the transgressions which

you have committed against me, and get
yourselves a new heart and a new spirit! Why
will you die, O house of Israel? For I have no
pleasure in the death of any one, says the
Lord God; so turn, and live' (Ezekiel 18.31-
32). The most graphic picture of the agony of
heart that judgment brings to God is seen in
Jesus sitting down and weeping over
Jerusalem because it would not come to Him
and be saved. The horror of Hell does not
delight God. If I may put it that way, it
makes Him cry.

Has it ever struck you, Paul, the way that
God showed His disapproval of the sin of
Nineveh in the book of Jonah? He was
provoked to judgment by the extent of the
wickedness there. It stank to Heaven. But His
reaction was not to pour out His wrath
immediately. Rather it was to plead with a
man to dare to be a missionary to them. A
delay was set on judgment — only forty days,
but that was enough. God gave them an
opportunity to hear and repent.

Peter, who as an ageing apostle had not at
all lost his expectation of the day of the Lord,
wrote of God's unwillingness to damn people
in the same terms. 'The Lord is not slow
about his promise (to come as judge) as some
count slowness, but is forbearing toward you,
not wishing that any should perish, but that
all should reach repentance' (2 Peter 3.9).
Judgment is delayed to give people more
chance to escape it.

Evidently there were people in the days of the apostles who argued just like the minister at the crematorium. They said that judgment was a wrong idea. The world had always been the same and would always remain the same. Peter said they deliberately ignored the facts about the flood, when God intervened in devastating judgment, just as He said He would. Therefore we may assume that He will keep His word about the judgment by fire.

So far there have been nearly twenty centuries in which the Lord has patiently waited in order to give folk opportunities to become Christians. Peter urged Christians to be 'hastening the coming of the day of God' (2 Peter 3.12). There are various things involved in this, but most people have reckoned that world evangelism is one of them. Jesus made it clear that the Gospel of the Kingdom was to be preached throughout the whole world, to all nations, before the end would come (Matt. 24.14, Mark 13.10). On His own word, He cannot return until the nations are properly evangelized.

Despite His personal trauma, Jesus prayed for His disciples' witness on the night before He was crucified. He longed that the world should know who He was, and that they should also know what a wonderful thing it is to be a Christian (John 17.21,23). So He prayed that God would bless His people. He knew that God had got to do something pretty remarkable to them if the world was to get the message! And He wanted the world to get the message, badly.

Now I think that this renewed sense of horror that has come to you in these sad days may in a way help you to begin to think and to be burdened as God is.

Because God longs for lost people to be converted, He seeks most of all to involve us in the work of prayer. Paul told young Timothy that hard work in prayer should be at the top of his daily agenda. But it wasn't to be the sort of selfish shopping list that we so easily lapse into! Timothy was to have a world vision in his prayer. He was to pray for people all over the place, and for governments and those in authority. The reason that was given for this was fundamentally evangelistic. Governments can help or hinder the work of the Gospel. You already know about the problems of missionary visas. You can appreciate the way that we pray and pray at election times in certain countries. There are political parties in Asia today that would make it extremely hard for the work of God's church if they were to come to power. So we are to pray for governments. And we are to pray for all people. This is because it is 'acceptable in the sight of God our Saviour, who desires all men to be saved and to come to the knowledge of the truth' (1 Timothy 2.1-4).

God wants people to be saved. Therefore God wants people to be prayed for.

A former colleague of mine, when he was a student at an Agricultural College, knew of no other Christians in the college. So he prayed that God would give him the names of twelve fellow students to pray for. Then he prayed for them every day. Before the year was out, there was a group of 13 Christians in that college!

It is not always as simple as that. But, as I have written to you before, there is plenty of encouragement in Scripture for us to pray for people to be converted, and to regard that as the primary work in evangelism.

Then, if we care like God, we should pray for workers.

Matthew wrote of a time when Jesus was deeply moved by the urgent needs of the cities and villages, especially the way the people were 'harassed and helpless, like sheep without a shepherd.' Jesus' reaction was to turn to His disciples and enlist their help . . . in prayer! 'The harvest is plentiful, but the labourers are few; pray therefore the Lord of the harvest to send out labourers into his harvest' (Matthew 9.35-38). I wonder when you last asked the Lord to send out a missionary into a particulary needy part of the world?

When my wife was first specially burdened about Asia, the Lord brought to her notice a number of her friends whom she believed ought also to be missionaries in Asia. She began to pray that the Lord would send each

one of them out. And they have all gone to
Asia. The last one left for Bhutan only last
year. She was prayed out for about sixteen
years! But she went.

God really does answer prayer for workers.
A student I was once talking to really came to
believe this. He said, 'I think the Lord is
calling me to be a missionary. But please
don't put me on your wife's prayer list!'

A few years back a small Christian group
was meeting to pray in Switzerland for OMF's
work in Asia. They were particularly praying
about the problem of some German-speaking
missionaries who had no German-speaking
teacher to instruct their children. Several
families working among tribal people would
probably have to abandon their work. As they
prayed one of their number looked up and
said, 'Ruth, you are a German-speaking
teacher. And you are free to go!' Somebody
else said, 'And we could support you' and so
Ruth came and did the job. Churches were
established among several different tribes
because a group prayed for a worker, and
God answered.

An American missionary once despaired
about the needs of high school students in
Mexico City. He just did not have the time to
reach them. So he prayed for a fellow-
American to come and work with him. One
day God seemed to ask him why he wanted
an American, and from that point on he
began to pray for a worker from anywhere in

the world.

The very day he changed his prayer, Miss Leni Sison, a colleague of ours in the Philippines, began to get the message about Mexico. After a week she came to my wife and said, 'Rose, do you think I'm crazy? I cannot get Mexico out of my mind. Do you think God could be calling me to go there?' We lent her magazines about Mexico and in time it was wonderfully confirmed that God was calling her there. She went, and fulfilled a ministry for which there was great need. A man prayed in Mexico City. God answered by speaking to a woman in Manila — just the person for the job.

Please join me in praying out the team of workers that we urgently need to buy up our present opportunities.

You know from bitter experience that time and opportunity run out . . .

I'm so glad that you have found a fiancée who can lift you up when you are down. She sounds a super girl. We are much looking forward to meeting her. Why don't the two of you come here for a break one weekend? We can fit you in somewhere, and this much maligned city of Glasgow has many delights to offer! We are only twenty minutes' drive from the shores of Loch Lomond. And you might even bring the sunshine with you and make it worth a visit there!

With Christian love,
DICK.

12

FACING HELL'S CHALLENGE

Dear Dick,

You're dead right. This experience of seeing somebody very precious to me die without trusting Jesus has made me see how urgent world evangelism is. I had accepted that before in theory. Now, I wonder how I could really spend my life in anything except in making the Gospel known to people while there still is a chance.

I have been reading through the book 'Operation World'.[1] You recommended it to me ages ago, but I've only just got round to reading it. In some ways I suppose that it is quite encouraging, because it does make it clear that there is an on-going Christian work almost everywhere in the world. But it is frightening to see just how many people have yet to be reached with the Gospel. The job is not done, and it is terribly urgent.

I want you to know that Rachel and I have been very earnestly praying about where the Lord wants us to go. As we have both had strong links with OMF over the years, we feel

[1] Published by *Send the Light*.

most naturally that we would like to serve in East Asia with you. But I don't know whether you have the sort of openings that would suit us. Some of your speakers seems to be rather high-powered types, and others I've met have all sorts of qualifications. I wonder whether there really are openings for ordinary people like us. Please could you drop me a line some time telling me some of the openings that you have in Asia at the moment. Rachel and I would like to pray over them together.

I was struck the other day in reading Dr Broomhall's new biography of Hudson Taylor. You know the way that Hudson Taylor could not get the mission-field out of his mind. He wrote around 1850, 'We are studying anatomy . . . when I feel tired of it, I think of China and the thought braces me up and I persevere. China is the subject of all my thoughts and prayers, at night many times when the others are sound asleep. I have not the slightest idea how I shall go, but this I know, I shall go . . . I know God has called me to the work, and He will provide the means.'[2] That is the sort of feeling I am getting these days. So often when I am at work it's this thought that crosses my mind. How long will it be before I can go and get on with mission work? Even when I am supposed to be studying in the evenings my mind often wanders to the same subject.

I don't think it's an unhealthy obsession. If

[2] Over the Treaty Wall, page 25.

people really are lost, then we ought to be preoccupied with it. So please can I have some straight advice on what I should do to prepare for missionary service. I read somewhere that OMF was committed to the speediest possible evangelization of East Asia. I want to get a move on!

It will be nice to take you up on your offer of a weekend in Glasgow. Have you got any weekends free in September? Perhaps you could check that, and then I'll phone you in a day or two and see what we can fix up. I hope those conferences that you were cramming for went off all right. I guess it must be easy to panic sometimes in your sort of work.

With love from us both,
PAUL.

Dear Paul,

What a joy to have a letter from a man enquiring about evangelistic work in East Asia! I sometimes despair of us men. When I first went to Asia, I attended the Mission's Orientation Course at our headquarters in Singapore. There were sixteen single lady missionaries on the course, and me! It was like living in a nunnery! (Actually there were four married couples as well. That only slightly improved the ratio.) It isn't as bad now but the imbalance is still there.

All sorts of sociological and other reasons are given for this imbalance in the missionary task force. I reckon they are excuses. And there is no doubt that we Christian men will be called to account if we fail to fulfil our calling and ministry.

Forgive me hopping on to one of my hobby-horses! But I do believe that we need urgently to pray men out into Asia. In some countries where we work we simply cannot accept any more single lady missionaries. In those cultures there are serious restrictions on the work of women, and we are in danger of planting women's meetings instead of churches! That is no criticism of the fantastic work that most of our girls do. Where there is imbalance it is not their fault, it's us men who must take the blame. So pray the men out!

I'm delighted to think that you might be one of them. And I am happy to send you the enclosed list of the many openings that we have for this year. You will notice that relatively few of them are for experts or specialists. They are for evangelists and disciple-makers: people whom the Lord has equipped to explain the Gospel to others and to help them on in their Christian lives when they get converted. It is the sort of work that you wrote of before when you shared your problems in explaining the Gospel to different Asian students. There is a difference however.

In most of our OMF situations, you cannot pass the buck of follow-up on to the local church. In many places there still isn't a local church. Therefore you need to be prepared, and perhaps trained, to 'plant' churches.

While it is true that the Lord has given OMF a few very gifted speakers, He has called many others to work with us who are not, and yet who are equally crucial.

I remember going for a walk in Manila with one of our missionaries. I don't think I have ever met anyone who talked so little in such a long time, and I couldn't help wondering how on earth he got on in pioneering Christian work in a tribal village. I later learned that it is the custom of that tribe to sit around for hours saying little or nothing. If I had gone into such a situation I would have put my foot in it right away, or had a nervous breakdown trying to keep quiet! As you know, sitting still and being quiet does not come naturally to me! It is a special gift that God has given to that missionary to reach that tribe.

When my wife first arrived in the Philippines somebody noticed that she was quieter and perhaps more introvert than I am. Not knowing that Rose had already had a fruitful ministry working among students in Britain, she told her that she did not know how she would manage to reach students in the Philippines, since she was shy and a relatively quiet person. 'Never mind', she said, 'After you've lived with Dick for a while you will probably change!' The fact is that Rosemary's quieter temperament has meant she has been able to reach all sorts of people whom I could never get near with my rather more boisterous personality.

I share this with you because I was concerned about the way you disparaged yourselves as 'ordinary people'. You are not ordinary on two counts. Firstly, because you are indwelt by the Spirit of God. That means that at the very least you are 'ordinary-plus'! But you are also not ordinary because God says you are special. You were chosen by Him with a particular work in His mind, which only you can properly fulfil. Since I have been here in Scotland we have sent out missionaries from all sorts of backgrounds — a nurse or two, a research chemist, one or two teachers, a plumber and an artist, a merchant seaman, a worker with the mentally handicapped, an engineer, and others. Most of them are now involved in evangelism in East Asia. The question is not 'What is your background or academic training?' It is, 'Has God called you to this particular work?'

And this is what I really want you and Rachel to think about. It is great that you have such a real burden for the lost. But that does not of itself constitute a missionary call. Paul had a tremendous burden for his fellow-countrymen. The burden lay so heavily on him that he described it as 'great sorrow and unceasing anguish in my heart' (Romans 9.1-

3). But he was not called as an apostle to the Jews. He was called to win Gentiles for Christ. The burden for a people did not constitute a call to them.

Nevertheless, Paul's burden for Jews did lead to action. But it was the work of prayer rather than the task of evangelism. Be sure that your burden leads to action too. Otherwise it is just pious emotionalism.

Some people think that the letter to the Romans was written as a text book for sound doctrine. But that was not the reason why it was written — it was written as an apologetic for missionary work. The whole doctrinal argument is an answer to the question, 'How is it that you feel obliged to take the Gospel to all sorts of people?' 'How is it that you are not ashamed to share the Gospel with anyone anywhere?'

I haven't time to take you through his doctrinal explanation now. You see, I hope to go to bed sometime tonight! But I do want you to notice what Paul *DID* because he was burdened for the nations. I think this might be a helpful guideline for you now that God has gripped you with the needs of lost people.

First of all, he got information about what God was doing in the world. Although Paul had not been to Rome, he knew a great deal about how the Italian Christians were getting on. He got letters, he consulted travellers, and he read widely. Why should a Jew brought up in Turkey be bothered about the

church in Italy? The answer is clear. He
believed that the wrath of God hung over
unconverted Italians. He wanted them to be
saved, so he wanted to know how the work
was progressing. Have you got that world map
on your wall yet? I remember our former
General Director, Mike Griffiths, telling us
about the missionary fellowship that he
belonged to when he was a student. It was
their aim to know something about
everywhere, and everything about somewhere.
That was a while ago, but I do not think it
can be bettered today.

Alongside the responsibility to get
information, Paul placed the urgent work of
prayer. I never cease to be amazed at the way
that he found time to work in prayer. And he
did not just pray for the work that he was
specially wrapped up in. He made time to
pray for the Italian church which he had never
seen (Romans 1.9).

Quite often when people come to me and
say that they have a burden for world mission,
I ask them which parts of the world they are
praying for. Too often the answer is
disappointing. But I believe you can tell a
person really cares by the way he prays. You
do not often get thanks for praying. But God
says that's the way to get things done.

There is a lot of preparation to be done
before you can work for God in East Asia. I
think you will need to get some Bible college
training. To teach and apply the Bible in

another language and a different culture needs
more skill than you have got through learning
to lead a small group Bible study. You would
be out of your depth without some sort of
training. Then you are going to have to spend
quite a lot of time in language study. Many
British people assume that if they speak
English loud enough everybody will
understand. But that is certainly not true in
most of the areas where we need evangelists
today. So it's going to be some years before
you can actually get down to the work you are
at present burdened to do.

But you can pray. And you must.

I believe that it's as we pray that God
focuses our thinking and our burden. How
about getting a few friends in to pray
together? Most of the OMF prayer groups
here are in the process of transferring to
Heaven, and younger groups are urgently
needed. Would it be too much to start a
monthly meeting?

There was one other element in the
outworking of Paul's burden which I think is
tremendously important for us. He looked for
openings for ministry (see Romans 1.11-15).
He knew of the spiritual need in Italy: he
asked God if he might have the privilege of
going (Romans 1.10). He was prepared to be
mobile for the sake of the Gospel. He
recognized that wanting to go wasn't the same
as a call, but he did ask for the privilege of
going. Indeed he tried to go, and he learned

about guidance when he was prevented from going (Romans 1.13).

Sometimes when people apply to missionary societies and are not accepted for service, members of their churches consider them as failures. Sometimes people even consider themselves failures. This is wrong. All that missionary councils and people like myself, together with ministers and elders, are really interested in is whether or not God has called a person to such and such a place. Luke recorded for us the fact that Paul and Timothy applied for service in the Province of Asia and then in Bithynia, but on both occasions the Spirit made it clear that that was not where they were to serve. Some people seem to imply that if they had been truly spiritual men they would not even have tried to go. But there is no hint in Luke's telling of the story (Acts 16.6-10) that they were out of touch with the Lord or spiritually rather suspect. The guidance came when they were prepared to go, and started going.

Do reckon to go for the sake of ministry and not simply to have a look around. One problem with the ease of modern travel has been the birth of missionary tourism. Some of the 19th century missionaries to Africa did not have a life expectancy of more than about eighteen months. But they went 'for life'. I have just driven a couple to the station who first went to China in 1928. Their commitment continues to be at the level expected in those days. This was their first furlough in Scotland for fourteen years.

The apostle Paul's conviction was that people needed the Gospel. He never thought in terms of settling down or of retiring to comfort. He did not give a year or two to the Lord's work — he gave his life to it. I am glad that you two seem to be prepared to follow in that tradition.

Another area that you might like to review is the matter of your finances. Now that you are planning to get married there may be a strong temptation to become very self-orientated in the way you spend or save your money. In a recent discussion on financing the work of the Gospel in our church we estimated how much it would cost fully to support the Christian workers we had sent out. When we divided the estimate by the number of active members in the congregation, we arrived at a guideline weekly sum for members who wanted to take seriously their giving for world evangelism. One friend commented, 'Each Friday night I spend more than that on ice cream and chocolate for the family. Surely world mission is worth more than ice cream and chocolate!'

That remark stuck with me. I had to review my priorities and see what items in my budget were given more importance than the evangelization of the world. It is an area in which it is foolish to be mean. We lose personally, and so does the work of God that we claim to be supporting.

Only since the Lord gave me the courage to take Him seriously on this matter have I been able to make ends meet!

Well, those are a few obvious practical ideas to help you review what you are doing at the moment. I'm glad that you are prepared to go as missionaries to Asia, and I very much hope that God will confirm that call. By the way, I hope that you have talked about this with the leaders of your home church. If you apply through me, I shall certainly want to know whether they agree with your sense of guidance. You would deserve to be pretty embarrassed if I asked their opinion and found that they didn't know what I was talking about! There are a lot of bridges to cross before you can start missionary work. But there's plenty that you can do, and ought to be doing, now.

When you next write I hope there will be some news of how you are getting on with it! As I have said to you before, to believe in Hell and do nothing is great wickedness. It's a sort of murder.

May the Lord continue to give you peace about what's past, clear guidance for your future, and the *oomph* really to do something here and now.

With much love from us all. Looking forward to your visit in September!

Yours sincerely,
DICK.

Epilogue

WHAT'S NOT FAIR?

My son David's favourite expression these days is 'it's not fair!' It's not fair that he can't stay up late. It's not fair if he has to do his homework before he goes out to play. It's not fair because Rachel didn't get a smack and he did. It's not fair because I had to go and preach and he wanted me to play football!

Sometimes he is right and we haven't been fair. Often it *is* fair but doesn't seem so when he thinks the world ought to revolve around him.

We live in a time when everybody is comparing himself with everybody else and saying 'It's not fair'. Nurses say it's not fair that they don't get as much money as school teachers. Teachers say it's not fair that they have not got the industrial clout of the miners. Various bodies have been formed whose responsibility it is to try and see that we are fair. The Equal Opportunities Commission works hard to try and see that everybody has the same chance regardless of sex, colour, or creed. I think we could do with an Equal Opportunities Commission to think about the problem of evangelism in the

world! When we shout 'God, that's not fair!'
we are often talking about things that are in
fact fair though they don't seem so from our
feeble perspective. I have tried to show that
God is not unfair in His dealings with
mankind. But God does not need me to
defend Him. He has stated the ways of His
justice and ultimately those ways will be
vindicated. You may not be persuaded by my
arguments, but when you meet God you will
be persuaded that He is perfectly fair in His
treatment of mankind.

But do *we* treat people fairly? Do we give
people equal opportunities to come to Christ?
Some time ago our Mission pulled out of
North-East Thailand. This was not because
the work was done: the church among the 15
million Thai who live in those districts is
virtually non-existent. But we just did not
have enough workers. No other Christian
mission works among the Thai in that area. Is
it fair that Britain should have 44,000
ministers for less than 60 million people when
North-East Thailand has none among 15
million?

Now of course there is great spiritual need
in Britain today and plenty of folk who as yet
have heard nothing of Jesus. But in terms of
equal opportunity there is simply no
comparison.

Not long ago in a Scottish village of 2,000
inhabitants the believers were praying for a
godly man to be called to the ministry of the

Word in one of the churches. A few hundred yards away was another congregation which already had a converted minister. That village now has two full-time Christian workers. I have no doubt that both of them are 'called' there. I love them dearly and pray for them often. But in terms of the deployment of manpower, I have to ask: Is it fair that 2,000 people should be ministered to full-time by two well-qualified Christian workers (and men at that!) while in the south of the Philippines the Maguindanao number over 650,000 and are still waiting for anyone to preach the Gospel clearly to them. Until recently no one had lived with them long enough to learn their language, let alone share the Gospel with them. We have been able to send one single lady to witness among them!

In that Scottish village there are several laymen who give a lively testimony to the Lord Jesus and are not ashamed to talk about Him with their workmates. In two-thirds of the towns and villages of Japan there are no Christians at all — and no missionaries to share the Gospel either!

When the people of God were in the wilderness God did not distribute the manna equally. Some gathered plenty; others found it rather thin on the ground. God designed the manna so that it would go bad if it were not eaten on the day it was collected. (The only exception to this was on Fridays when a supply was given for Friday and Saturday, so that the people of God could observe the day of rest.) God's purpose in this unequal distribution seems to have been to encourage the give and take of sharing within the people of God. Manna that was stockpiled went rotten in their hands. (See Exodus 16.14-20 and 2 Corinthians 8.13-15).

In these days God has not equally distributed gifts and personnel to His church. In some parts of the world He has given much, in others little. But if these gifts are not shared they stagnate and become rotten. It grieves me to see gifted Christians stockpiled in some of our churches. They have gifts of ministry that are so little used. Is it any wonder that our churches are stagnant? Many Christians sitting in rows of pews are 'going mouldy' when their gifts are urgently needed in other spiritually deprived parts of the world!

We so easily get sidetracked on to secondary issues. A study group within my own Presbytery was formed because of concern at the amount of money being spent on maintaining church buildings. The Committee's burden was to 'ensure that the first priority of the church remains the work of Mission, and not the maintenance of property'. How that priority needs to be guarded! I have lost count of the ministers who have told me that when their new church building project is completed they hope to turn their attention to the whole business of world missions. The implication is clear. Many congregations are spending their energy and their income on beautiful buildings for their comfortable worship. That is not the priority of Jesus. He left the comfort of the worship of heaven and was prepared to have no place to lay His head, if only people could find eternal salvation.

In this book we have looked at some of the most frightening Scriptures. My burden is that the Church should regain its primary responsibility of taking the Gospel to the nations. We are saved for worship and for evangelism: for worship because that is what God most fundamentally deserves, and for evangelism because that is what the church most fundamentally needs (1 Peter 2.5,9). If you have read this far then I must ask you one important question: what are you going to do about it? The biblical material demands action — not a discussion group. I was speaking the other week at the Truth and Liberation Church in Melbourne, Australia. Towards the close of the meeting the minister asked the congregation what they were going to do about what they had heard. Several were clearly quite shattered by the challenge of world mission. One suggested that the speakers should return the following Sunday so that there could be more discussion with more people in the congregation informed. Then another commented, 'We do not need more discussion. We *know* what we've got to do. Let's get on and do it!' He was right.

Some of you will be tempted to use your disagreement with me over an odd point here and there as an excuse for inaction. I urge you rather to let the weight of the Scriptures discussed grip your mind and lead you to action. People are in urgent need of the Gospel. Let's not fiddle around in the luxury of people quibbling!

We must pray out labourers.

We must commit ourselves to wrestling in prayer for the lost.

We must share the Gospel now — and seek to learn to do it better.

We must invest in world evangelism — with the sort of sacrifice that shows we believe it is urgent.

We must look for those to go where people don't have a fair chance of hearing the Gospel. Perhaps (probably?) you should try to go yourself!

Is that asking too much? Is that 'not fair'? Doesn't a lost world demand such sacrifice? Doesn't the Lord Jesus, our Saviour, deserve such devotion?

**GOVERNMENT OF INDIA
ARRIVAL CARD**

(Rules 5 & 16 of Registration of Foreigners Rules)

8. Purpose of visit (put √ in appropriate box)

Tourism	Business	Transit	Official	Employment	Education	Conference	Social	Medical Treatment	Pilgrimage	Sports	Other

9. Address in India

Hebron School - 643 001
Ooctacamund Tamil Nadu.

Telephone number 423 2442372

Immigration Stamp

Incredible India

Welcome to India

1. Ministry... Home Affairs – *mha.nic.in* 2. Bureau of Immigration – *www.immigrationindia.nic.in*
3. Airport Authority of India – *www.airportsindia.org.in* 4. Central Board of Excise & Customs
– *www.cbec.gov.in* 5. Ministry of Tourism – *www.incredibleindia.org.in*, *www.tourism.nic.in*

IMPORTANT INSTRUCTIONS

A. It is obligatory for disembarking passengers to declare details of plants / plant material in their baggage on arrival in India

B. REGISTRATION FORMALITIES FOR FOREIGN NATIONALS

1. If you are entering India on a student, Employment, Research, Medical or Missionary VISA, which is valid for more than 180 days, you are required to register with the Foreigners Registration Officer under whose jurisdiction you propose to stay. This should be done within 14 days of arrival in India, irrespective of your actual period of stay.

2. Foreigners visiting India on any other category of long term VISA that is valid for more than 180 days, are not required to register themselves **if their actual stay does not exceed 180 days** on each visit. If such a foreigner intends to stay in India for more than 180 days during a particular visit, he/she should get registered within 180 days of arrival in India.

3. The following categories of foreign nationals are exempt from registration:

   (a) Those visiting India on any short term VISA i.e. valid for 180 days or less.

   (b) Children below 16 years of age. (irrespective of any type of VISA)

   (c) Holding VISA for Overseas Citizen of India (OCI)

4. Pakistan nationals are required to register within 24 hours of their arrival in India. Afghanistan nationals are required to register within 7 days of their arrival in India.

C. INFORMATION REGARDING CUSTOMS

Indian Customs requires you to declare goods in excess of the free allowance, prohibited or restricted ... Wildlife